641.59
AFRICA
Timothy
$35

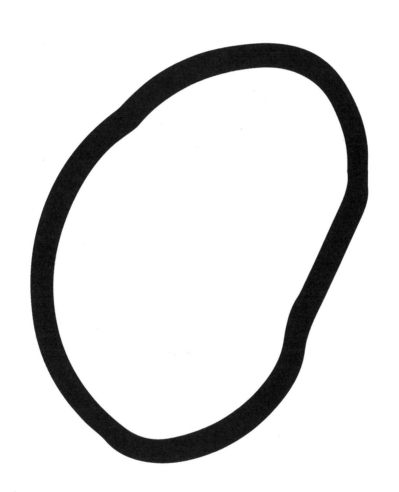

FOOD FROM ACROSS AFRICA

FOOD FROM ACROSS AFRICA

Duval Timothy
Jacob Fodio Todd
Folayemi Brown

Photography by Toby Glanville & Sophie Davidson
Illustration by Duval Timothy

An Imprint of HarperCollinsPublishers

Family in Ghana, Nigeria, Sierra Leone, Kenya and South Sudan connect us to Africa, though south London is the landscape that brings us together. It provides the markets where we shop and the spaces where we host our dinners. It's the place we call home.

Looking back, we didn't think twice before launching The Groundnut. It was the perfect thing to pursue at that moment in time. This book is a retrospective that represents the first nine menus we came up with and the history behind the recipes. Even the very simplest dish underwent hours of deliberation for an event, and then again, to make it into this book.

We aim to make food that is simple, balanced, beautiful and fundamentally to share.

Introduction

In January 2012 we started a bimonthly supper club called The Groundnut. The evenings featured the food of our childhoods, especially our heritage in West and East Africa. The aim we had in mind was to draw attention to traditional recipes, both inherited and adapted, as well as to explore new ingredients and combinations. African food is some of the best on the planet. It is easily shopped for and cooked, yet remains for some reason off the culinary radar of most people in Britain. We want to change that.

Each evening our thirty-four guests are welcomed with a cocktail and plantain crisps, followed by a relaxed multiple-course meal. We change the menu from event to event, but in our repertoire are any number of classic African dishes, many of which have been passed down through generations: from the fragrant and ubiquitous West African dish, jollof rice, to innovative modern offerings like our aromatic star anise and coconut chicken served in a steaming plantain leaf.

All the evenings in 2012 were hosted on two long tables in the beautiful St. John's Hall, an eighteenth-century registered landmark building near Tower Bridge and one of the few remaining watch houses in the country. In July 2013 we hosted over 200 people over seven days in a South London gallery space, Lewisham Arthouse, and our evenings at Le Bal Café in Paris filled up just a week after tickets were made available. We have since returned for another run at Lewisham Arthouse, and hosted periodic events out of our studio in Deptford while developing the recipes for this book. The venture is self-financed and every evening up until now has sold out completely.

After two years of putting on these public events we have identified demand, great support, and incredible curiosity about the food we make and the way we present it. Initially we sold tickets predominantly to family and friends but along the way we have accumulated a lengthy mailing list, and some loyal customers.

Collectively we have spent time living, working, and visiting family in Africa—in the Southeast, Swaziland to South Sudan, and in the West, predominantly Sierra Leone and Nigeria—although for many years we have been based in South London. It is where we all met, where we all live, and where The Groundnut went from being an idea discussed around our kitchen tables to being a fully formed and successful enterprise. The local markets in Deptford, Brixton, East Street, and Lewisham are also where we shop for the majority of our ingredients.

We want to introduce new foods and explain where and how to source them. We expect to present ways of eating that people may not have previously experienced and to change the way that commonly available ingredients are approached, in such a way that the possibilities when undertaking a weekly shop will expand inestimably.

Our food is communal in the sense that a lot of it is prepared with sharing in mind. At our evenings, food is distributed banquet style: in big dishes passed down tables, in edible bowls, or wrapped in plantain leaves that guests have to delicately unfurl. Our food encourages tactility, with influences from our childhoods growing up eating freshly picked mangoes sprinkled with salty chili powder, being served juice in a peeled, cored, and squeezed orange and hand rolling and dunking balls of eba into okra soup then straight into your mouth.

The food is associative in the way that our recipes fit together, and interact with one another in menus. Instead of making explicit distinction by chapters between starters, mains, and desserts we have structured the book by menus to represent the way that dishes fit together, whether attached by season, dominant flavors, or by another unifying point of inspiration.

menu

"Groundnut stew is a dish to be shared with others—it's one of the things that best represents what our dinners are about."

Soon after deciding to embark on The Groundnut, we went on holiday to Vienna for our friend Denis's birthday. Staying at the Kabwa's family home, with Mama cooking for us, was emotional, and the food, music, and company created a beautiful atmosphere around the table. It was a timely reminder of why we were about to share the food of Sub-Saharan Africa and its diaspora. After two rounds of hugs, we returned to London with inspiration and plum brandy.

We announced dates for our first dinners and instantly spent most of the money we'd invested in cutlery. At that point we knew there was no going back. If we hadn't had to pay for those knives, forks, and spoons, who knows what we would have been up to now. We're hoping they will start to turn a profit sometime soon.

Yemi travelled to Nigeria, and when he returned, preparations got intense. Perhaps the most important things we needed were tables. Roughly a year beforehand I had taken one of my large paintings off the wall in the flat and used it as a tabletop for a dinner with friends. It worked surprisingly well, so I was confident we could design and build our own tables. The wooden table tops were stretched tightly with red felt fabric. For each subsequent set of dinners we would restretch them with a different-colored fabric in relation to the theme of the dinner, the space, and our food. The color of the tables quickly became an important factor in determining the mood in the evening.

For the first dinner, there was so much groundwork for us to overcome that when it came to creating the menu, we relied on a favorite traditional dish that always impresses—groundnut—a rich stew made with peanut butter, onions, and aromatic Scotch bonnet peppers. It's so good that Yemi says if he eats it, he might die. Really. Groundnut stew is a dish to be shared with others—it's one of the things that best represents what our dinners are about, even taking into account Yemi's peanut allergy.

Each of our menus is created around a centerpiece that forms a theme that ties everything together. We wanted to complement the groundnut with light and simple dishes such as radish, green beans, and ugali, to create a well-balanced meal that highlights the qualities of each dish on the table.

Across West Africa, oranges are skillfully peeled on the street. They're sold to people who drink the juice from a hole at the top of the fruit, and the orange functions as both the cup and the drink. Peeling the fruit makes the skin more malleable and easier to squeeze without it splitting. Each roadside vendor will often have a modest setup selling just oranges.

Through repetition, they have mastered the technique of elegantly spiraling around the entire surface of each orange with a sharp knife in a matter of seconds. The often beautifully arranged pyramids of oranges and the fresh aroma of citrus from the ongoing peeling draws attention to these humble stalls. The yellow, orange, and reddish colors of citrus fruits supposedly develop during cool winters. In tropical regions, cool winters don't exist in the same way, so you might commonly drink from a green orange.

This orange juice is as fresh as it gets and a lot of fun to drink. Most types of orange will work, but try to choose firm oranges with a bit of give. In general the heavier the orange is, the juicier it will be.

ORANGE JUICE

**Serves 4
(one orange per person)
Time: 4 minutes per orange**

4 oranges

Peel the orange starting from the top, using a small sharp knife or vegetable peeler to remove all the skin and leaving the white pith intact. When peeling, try to remove an equal amount of skin around the entire orange. *Any deep cuts will cause the orange to fracture and juice might squirt out of the wrong part when you drink.*

Cut a ¾-inch-wide hole at the top of the orange and remove the core at the top of the fruit. With a small knife, pierce the flesh of the orange in a few places through the hole at the top, making sure not to pierce the skin anywhere. *Doing this ensures that when you squeeze the orange, the juice will push out through the middle of the orange and up to the drinking hole rather than potentially splitting the skin.*

To drink, put your mouth to the hole in the orange and suck the juice while gently squeezing the fruit. Squeeze the fruit evenly around its surface as you continue to drink until no more juice is released. Once you have squeezed the juice, you can rip the fruit apart and enjoy the flesh.

For some reason, the making of plantain chips always falls to me—I thought—because of my unrivaled chopping technique, and a beautiful knife. A year and thousands of chips later, we purchased a mandoline (a cooking utensil used to finely cut in bulk at speed). Yet . . . the task continues to burden me alone. Yemi and Duval's praise for my mandoline skills does not wash.

The truth is, it is a job that requires patience, with only a few repetitive stages. On the upside we've learned a great deal about how to produce the very best plantain chips. There is no need to make them fresh, as we misguidedly attempted for our first few events, because if sealed properly they keep well for up to two weeks. We advise using only the greenest green plantain to achieve a consistent outcome, which will be crunchy, slightly sweet chips that are hard to stop eating once one has started, much like potato chips, for which they are substitutes in many areas of the world.

GREEN PLANTAIN CHIPS

Serves plenty

Time: 1 hour

3 green plantains

2 quarts sunflower oil

1 teaspoon sea salt (or to taste)

Top and tail the plantains and slice down the spine. Forcefully but carefully remove the skin, using the side of a small knife to lift it and then your thumb joint to coax it off. *Keep an eye on your fingernail, as plantain skin under the nail can be painful.*

Finely slice the plantain (using a knife or mandoline) into round chips, about 1/16 inch thick, and drop them into a tub of cold water. Try to ensure they do not get any more than a generous 1/8 inch thick.

Heat the oil to 375°F.

Remove the discs from the water, drain in a colander, and pat dry with paper towels so that they do not spit when they go into the hot oil.

Deep-fry the chips in batches, a handful at a time, cooking for 2–4 minutes, or until the chips begin to brown. They color further on removal, so remove them just as they take on a brownish hint. Place them on a dish lined with paper towels to remove excess oil and pat with paper towels.

Allow to rest, remove the paper towels, and season with the sea salt. *It is good to season the chips while they are still hot, as then the salt sticks to them.*

To store, put into a sealed bag or Tupperware container with a good seal. They last up to 2 weeks—or at least that's the longest that we've managed to keep them uneaten.

Depending on the type of pomegranate and its ripeness, the seeds will vary in size, quantity, and color, ranging from pale pink to deep purple. For this recipe, the sweetness of very ripe, dark seeds works well against the slight bitterness of the eggplant. To find a good pomegranate, look for a fruit with a dry skin and slightly wonky concave sides. Perfectly round pomegranates need a few days to ripen.

EGGPLANT & POMEGRANATE

Serves 4

Time: 50 minutes

2 eggplants

2 tablespoons cumin seeds

8 black peppercorns

1 tablespoon ground ginger

½ teaspoon salt

½ cup olive oil

1 large pomegranate, or 2 small ones

Preheat the oven to 390°F.

Slice off the stems of the eggplants and halve each one lengthwise. Slice each eggplant half diagonally into ¼-inch-wide strips and place on a large rimmed baking sheet. If necessary, use two baking sheets so that the eggplant slices do not overlap each other.

Using a pestle and mortar, thoroughly crush the cumin seeds and whole peppercorns with the ground ginger and salt. *Mixing all the seasonings together before adding to the eggplant helps to evenly distribute flavor.*

Add the seasonings to your baking sheet(s). Using your hands, mix the eggplant strips with the seasonings until evenly covered. Add the olive oil and mix well. Place in the oven for 15 minutes. If you're using two baking sheets, swap them around halfway through cooking so that the eggplant cooks evenly.

Halve the pomegranate and extract all the seeds.

After 15 minutes, take the baking sheet(s) out of the oven and gently turn over each slice of eggplant using a spatula. *The eggplant will be quite moist and delicate at this stage.* Make sure the slices are not overlapping and put back into the oven for another 15 minutes. The eggplant should be browning slightly. Keep the slices in the oven for another 3–4 minutes. They are ready when well browned but still tender.

Toss the eggplant with the pomegranate seeds and add salt to taste. Serve hot.

GREEN BEANS & SESAME

Serves 4
Time: 10 minutes

2 tablespoons sesame seeds

¾ pound green beans

1 teaspoon toasted sesame oil

sea salt flakes, to taste

Put the sesame seeds into a small pan and dry-fry over medium heat for 2 minutes, shaking the pan occasionally. Once the seeds are golden brown, remove from the heat and put to one side.

Bring a pan of water to a boil. Meanwhile, wash the green beans and top and tail them. Boil the green beans for 2 minutes, then drain in a colander.

Put the beans into a bowl, add the sesame oil and the sesame seeds, and toss. Sprinkle with sea salt to taste.

*The value of sliced radishes as part of a meal should not be underestimated.
We use them to add color, texture, and freshness to a meal and they are also an
easy, nutritious snack. We often serve them alongside the groundnut, which highlights
how crisp and refreshing the cold radishes are, while the radishes emphasize how rich and
comforting the groundnut is. Radishes vary in size, shape, color, and peppery flavor,
but they are all light and crunchy. Look for ones that are firm, and try to use them
within a couple of days because they can become increasingly bitter over time.*

*If your radishes still have the leaves attached and they are in good condition,
you can keep them on, as they are edible and make a nice accompaniment.*

RADISHES

To serve four, wash a big bunch of radishes in cold water and shake well. Trim the root
of each radish. If you are not using the leaves, trim the top where the radish meets
the stem. Halve each radish from top to bottom and place in a bowl to share.

GRANDMA TIMOTHY

Groundnut stew is a West African peanut-based dish that you won't forget once you've tasted it. They serve something similar called chicken amendoins in Mozambique, where I spent some of my childhood. Yet when I left Maputo at six I didn't taste the dish, or anything like it, for another fifteen years. It was just a distant memory.

All until Duval's brother, Miles, brought it back into my life during our university days in New Cross. Little did I know, but the Groundnut stew is one of their grandma's trademark Sierra Leonean dishes, and when he was cooking it down I could smell something special happening. I gave it a little sample and actually couldn't believe it. I was immediately transported back to being a five-year-old in Maputo. I remember chatting with Duval and Yemi about it incessantly, genuinely excited, and I guess those lively exchanges form the basis of why we started The Groundnut together.

The Groundnut stew will always hold a special significance. It was the dish we chose to serve at our first event because it never seems to fail to impress people, and it is the dish that kindly lent us its name.

THE GROUNDNUT STEW

Serves 6

Time: 1 hour 30 minutes

1 chicken, skinned and chopped into 8 pieces

2 teaspoons salt

½ teaspoon ground black pepper

1 teaspoon white pepper

5 tablespoons peanut oil

1 Scotch bonnet pepper

4 small onions

3 cloves of garlic

2 heaping tablespoons tomato paste

½ cup homemade groundnut butter (see page 316), or smooth peanut butter

2 cups chicken stock (see page 314)

Place the chicken pieces into a large bowl, add the salt, black pepper, and white pepper, and mix well.

In a wide frying pan, fry the chicken with 3 tablespoons of peanut oil over medium heat. The chicken should not overlap, as this will prevent it from browning. If you are using a small pan, fry the chicken in batches.

Pierce the Scotch bonnet pepper with a sharp knife and add it to the pan. *Piercing the pepper means that as the stew develops it absorbs the flavor of the pepper, but if it becomes too spicy it can be removed at any point.*

Shake the pan regularly so that the chicken does not stick. Turn over after 5 minutes. While the chicken is browning, finely dice the onions and crush the garlic to a paste. Keep separate and put to one side.

After 5 minutes, add half the garlic to the pan and fry for another 5 minutes, so that the garlic and chicken brown together. *When given room in the pan, garlic caramelizes very quickly—this gives a lovely rich flavor and texture that attaches itself to the chicken.* When the chicken has browned nicely on both sides, remove it from the pan and put to one side.

Using the same pan, slightly increase the heat to medium-high and add the diced onions and the other 2 tablespoons of peanut oil. Cook the onions for 12 minutes, stirring regularly. When they are very soft and dark, turn the heat down to medium and add the tomato paste and the remaining garlic. Mix well and cook for 5 minutes, then add the groundnut butter and stir.

Put the browned chicken back into the pan and add the stock slowly while stirring, so that it is incorporated with the sauce. Leave to cook on a low heat for 25 minutes, stirring occasionally. It should reduce slightly and take on a thicker consistency. Serve hot.

In West Africa, the seeds of the egusi melon are a common component of the soups that are integral to daily life. Coarsely ground up, they thicken stews, adding texture and another layer of flavor. Egusi soup is usually prepared with fish and/or meat, but given its nutritional profile—the seeds are composed of mostly natural fats and protein—it works perfectly as a vegetarian alternative to the Groundnut stew.

CHICKPEA EGUSI

Serves 4

Time: 40 minutes

3½ ounces whole egusi seeds

3 medium onions

1 tablespoon olive oil

1 Scotch bonnet pepper

3 cloves of garlic

3 teaspoons salt

¾ pound plum tomatoes

1 tablespoon tomato paste

½ teaspoon dark brown sugar

2 teaspoons black pepper

1 teaspoon hot paprika

¼ teaspoon smoked paprika

scant 1 cup vegetable stock
or water

1 large red bell pepper

½ pound baby plum tomatoes

2½ cups cooked chickpeas

10 ounces baby spinach

1 tablespoon extra virgin olive oil

Preheat the oven to 350°F.

Roast the egusi seeds on the middle rack of the oven for 12 minutes, turning once. *The egusi should be crunchy and some will have taken on a golden brown color.* Remove from the oven and grind half the seeds with a pestle and mortar. Leave the rest whole and set all the seeds aside.

To make the base sauce, finely dice the onions and, in a large frying pan, gently fry in the oil for 5 minutes over medium heat. Seed and finely dice the Scotch bonnet pepper. Chop the garlic and crush to a paste with 1 teaspoon of salt. Add both to the pan and cook for another 10 minutes over low heat.

Chop the tomatoes and add to the pan with the tomato paste and dark brown sugar. Stir and taste. It should have a pleasant sweetness from the tomatoes, onions, and sugar, with a spicy undercurrent from the Scotch bonnet pepper. Add the black pepper, paprikas, and the other 2 teaspoons of salt.

Pour in the stock or water, then cover and simmer over low heat for 20 minutes. This allows the flavors to meld together. Remove from the heat and blend the base sauce. Taste and add more salt if necessary.

Add the ground egusi to the base. Simmer over low heat, uncovered, for 5 minutes. *The sauce should thicken and become a creamier color as the seeds absorb liquid.*

Rinse the bell pepper, then remove the stem and seeds. Cut it into ¼-inch squares. Quarter the baby plum tomatoes.

Then add the chickpeas, bell pepper, and baby plum tomatoes to the base and simmer for a final 5 minutes. Remove from the heat and add the spinach and the extra virgin olive oil. Serve just as the spinach begins to wilt, and scatter the reserved whole egusi seeds on top.

Ugali is a staple made of white cornmeal eaten across much of East Africa. It is one of those everyday dishes that growing up you might not care for—I didn't. There are cousins of this dish made with different grains across the continent (eba made from cassava, pounded yam, and fufu from a multitude of starchy crops).

It wasn't until as an adult my cousin Kate started regularly cooking cornmeal for me that I came to appreciate it properly. In her version the cornmeal is left to cook for longer and is softer and plumper than what I was accustomed to. I favor it as an accompaniment to the Groundnut stew. These days I still make it weekly or so, and I find it real comfort food. Roll ugali into small balls with your hands and then use to scoop sauce into your mouth.

UGALI

Serves 6

Time: 40 minutes

3 cups fine white cornmeal

Mix 1½ cups of cornmeal with a generous 2 cups of cold water in a deep saucepan. Put the saucepan over medium-low heat. Stir the cornmeal and water until well mixed, then add 5 cups of boiling water and continue stirring until it reaches the boiling point. *The liquid should start to thicken, taking on the consistency of porridge, and small air bubbles should slowly form on the surface.*

Cover the pan, leaving a small gap for steam to escape, and leave gently bubbling for 10 minutes over low heat. Now gradually add the remaining cornmeal, stirring frequently with a thick wooden spoon for 3 minutes until it is well mixed. *The amount of cornmeal you add at this point may vary depending on how fast it is cooking. The aim is to achieve a solid substance but with a fair bit of give, as it continues to cook.*

Leave over low heat for another 10 minutes, until the ugali has a slightly solid consistency. It will wobble a little when you shake the pan but should be solid.

Fill a large bowl with cold water. Place a serving spoon in the bowl. Using the spoon, make a scoop of ugali and put it on a flat plate. It will be extremely hot at first and will firm up as it cools. Repeat this process, putting the spoon back into the cold water each time before making another scoop.

Allow to cool for a few minutes, then serve.

For years I thought pomelos and grapefruits were one and the same. In fact, after a trip to Lagos I think we all spent a good while raving about this mythical African grapefruit, until Jacob's mum brought us dreamers back to earth by telling us what it was. There's something stately about this fruit. The jewels of flesh evoke an image of grandeur, but ultimately, this one is a fruit of your labor.

POMELO

To prepare, halve the pomelo with a serrated knife. Pressing firmly with your thumbs, peel and separate the pomelo from the white pith. It's notoriously deep and tough, so be patient with it. We want the clusters, or individual gems, within each segment that are roughly the same size as a grain of rice.

Enjoy as a bittersweet salad beside the main course or as a simple dessert.

YORKSHIRE PUDDING WITH MANGO CURD

Makes 12

Time: 1 hour 10 minutes

For the mango curd

1 large ripe mango

juice of 2 limes

2 egg yolks

¼ teaspoon salt

3½ tablespoons superfine sugar

5 tablespoons cold unsalted butter, cut into cubes

For 12 individual Yorkshire puddings

generous ¾ cup whole milk

scant ½ cup water

¾ cup all-purpose flour

1 tablespoon superfine sugar

¼ teaspoon salt

2 eggs

2 tablespoons sunflower oil (or another oil with a smoking point above 425°F)

To garnish

2 cardamom pods

a handful of pistachios

To make the mango curd, peel the mango and remove as much flesh from the pit as possible. Purée with a blender, then pass through a fine-mesh sieve to remove any fibrous strands. Add the lime juice.

Bring a medium pan half filled with water to a gentle simmer. Place the egg yolks, salt, and sugar in a bowl that will fit comfortably over the pan without falling in or touching the water. Whisk together until well combined. Add the mango purée mixture.

Place the bowl over the simmering water and cook for 12 minutes, stirring regularly with a wooden spoon to prevent the egg from scrambling.

Remove the curd from the heat and quickly whisk in the cold butter until it has completely dissolved, leaving the curd rich, creamy, and glossy. Put into a sterilized jar and refrigerate. Use when cold.

To make the Yorkshire puddings, pour the whole milk and water into a measuring cup. Place the flour, sugar, and salt in a mixing bowl. Add the eggs, then gradually add half the liquid from the measuring cup and whisk until smooth. Add the rest of the liquid and whisk until well combined.

Leave the batter to rest at room temperature for 15 minutes. *This raises the temperature of the mix, which allows the puddings to cook through to the center without burning.*

Preheat the oven to 425°F. Evenly spread the oil across the cups of a muffin tin, ensuring that each one is well greased. There should be a little pool of oil at the bottom of each cup. Place the empty tin on the top rack of the oven for at least 5 minutes.

Working quickly, remove the muffin tin from the oven and fill each cup with batter to come three-quarters of the way up. *You should hear a sizzle as the batter lands in the pool of hot oil. This is a good sign!* Put the muffin tin back into the oven and set a kitchen timer to 18 minutes. Do not open the oven door to check on the puddings, as this will disturb the temperature. After 18 minutes, take them out and leave them in the pan to cool.

Crush the cardamom pods and remove the small seeds. Crush a handful of pistachios with the seeds of cardamom until they form a fine powder.

Once the mango curd has set and the Yorkshire puddings have cooled down, generously fill the center of each pudding with the curd and sprinkle with the nut and cardamom mix.

menu

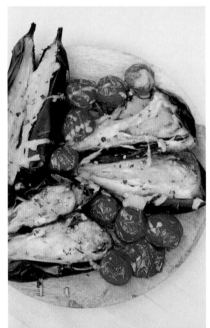

"Coffee, talk, music, chopping plantain, and kneading dough. Then Yemi's arrival at the kitchen, like that of a tornado."

The Groundnut's first home was St. John's Hall. It's an amazing building a few steps away from the south end of Tower Bridge, tucked away between a park and a church. The Georgian building, with a style reminiscent of Hawksmoor, has an interesting history. The warden of a cemetery, which has since become the park, previously inhabited it. Duval's parents bought the building in the eighties and used it as their architecture practice for years. Fortunately for us at the time, one of the large rooms adjacent to the kitchen was undergoing a fallow period, and whether Arthur Timothy was feeling particularly generous or was artfully persuaded, we are grateful that he permitted us to rent it for a few nights every two months to turn it into a restaurant.

In the run-up it was always a huge job turning the space around, with all the cleaning, and installing tables and chairs, and dressing the room. We'd refashion the narrow kitchen at St. John's Hall, which has shelved walls that run all the way up to a very high ceiling. The highest shelves would support pots, sculptures and other dusty, curious objects that would be evacuated from the shelves that were in easy reach, where we'd install our crockery, cutlery, and serving equipment. We'd always be criminally sleep-deprived in those days—however, it always seemed to be a pleasure to return to the kitchen in the morning after the first evening to start over. Coffee, talk, music, chopping plantain, and kneading dough. Then Yemi's arrival at the kitchen, like that of a tornado. Tin foil, plastic containers, stick blenders, and huge SportsDirect shopping bags start to fly around every possible surface as we scramble for cover. As the storm subsides, a beautifully crafted vegetarian dish can usually be spotted floating out of the kitchen supported by the heel of Yemi's hand.

GRAPEFRUIT TODDY

Makes about 2½ cups, enough for four drinks

Time: 30 minutes

4 grapefruits

10 cloves

1 cinnamon stick

2 tablespoons golden syrup

5 fluid ounces Scotch whisky

Peel the grapefruits, keeping the skin. Halve each grapefruit and squeeze the juice. Each one should provide roughly ½ cup of juice.

Put the grapefruit juice, grapefruit skins, cloves, cinnamon stick, and golden syrup into a bowl and leave to steep for 20 minutes.

Strain the liquid through a sieve. Add 1 cup of boiling water and the whisky and stir.

Pour the drink into glasses and serve warm.

We're accustomed to the word "soup" being used interchangeably with meat- and vegetable-laden stews or sauces that serve as an accompaniment to a staple, such as eba or pounded yam. This recipe has been tweaked to just a liquid soup, which works to whet the appetite and isn't too filling. We add a stalk of celery for scooping and crunching. For a more traditional version, see the Groundnut stew (page 33).

GROUNDNUT SOUP

Serves 4

Time: 1 hour 10 minutes

2 onions

1 large carrot

4 celery stalks

3 tablespoons peanut oil

½ teaspoon white pepper

1 Scotch bonnet pepper

1 tablespoon tomato paste

2 tablespoons peanut butter

4 cups hot vegetable or chicken stock (see pages 313, 314)

½ teaspoon sea salt flakes

a pinch of black pepper

Finely dice the onions, carrot, and 2 of the celery stalks.

Heat the peanut oil in a large nonstick heavy-bottomed pan. Add the diced onions, carrot, and celery, the white pepper, and Scotch bonnet (pierced with a sharp knife to ensure that the flavors seep out steadily) and cook over medium heat for 15 minutes, stirring at least every 5 minutes.

Add the tomato paste and cook for another minute. Stir in the peanut butter and leave to cook for another minute.

Now add the stock—it's important to add it gradually, stirring all the time. *This helps the elements in the soup to meld well.* Once all the stock has been added, cover with a lid and cook for 40 minutes, stirring occasionally.

Remove the Scotch bonnet pepper before blending with a hand blender for 2–3 minutes. Aim not to blend too heavily, as the soup can become too creamy (for our liking…).

Top and tail the other 2 celery stalks, then, using a vegetable peeler, nick the ends and pull out any thick fibers. Pour the soup into bowls, then halve the celery stalks and place one in each bowl, resting on the edge. Sprinkle with the sea salt and black pepper.

Serve hot.

This is a truly fantastic and simple way to cook okra. It doesn't get slimy in the way that puts many people off, but you get a real sense of the flavor of okra enhanced by lime and honey.

PAN-FRIED OKRA

Serves 4
Time: 10 minutes

¾ pound okra

2 tablespoons chili oil

¼ teaspoon salt

½ lime

1 heaping teaspoon honey

Wash the okra, trim the top of the pods and the very tips (although not the entire end), and dry with paper towels. Halve each okra lengthwise.

Heat the chili oil in a large frying pan over medium-high heat. Add the okra and cook for 3 minutes, stirring frequently, until it has softened slightly with some dark patches and has begun to wilt slightly.

Remove from the heat, add the salt, squeeze over the lime juice, and drizzle with the honey.

Toss and serve hot.

A Sudanese dip made with mashed eggplant and peanuts inspired this dish. The texture and flavor of a freshly roasted eggplant is unique, and it always seems a shame to mash it. This recipe is simple to prepare and preserves the combination of flavors. It can be served as a light starter or as a side dish.

ROASTED EGGPLANT & TOMATO WITH PEANUT SAUCE

Serves 4

Time: 50 minutes

4 large eggplants

2 tablespoons peanut butter

3½ tablespoons lemon juice

1 teaspoon ground cumin

1 teaspoon honey

1 teaspoon salt

2 tablespoons olive oil

½ pound tomatoes, on the vine

a handful of salted peanuts, crushed

Preheat the oven to 425°F.

Pierce each eggplant a few times with a fork, then place them on a baking sheet and put into the oven for 45 minutes, turning every 15 minutes. Alternatively, you can roast the eggplants over an open flame until the skin is well charred and the flesh is soft and tender.

Meanwhile, put the peanut butter, lemon juice, cumin, honey, and salt into a bowl and mix until well combined. Stir in the olive oil, then set aside.

After the eggplants have been in the oven for 35 minutes, add the tomatoes to the baking sheet. Leave for another 10 minutes, then remove both eggplants and tomatoes from the oven—the skin on the eggplants should be brittle and the flesh soft. Halve each eggplant, then place on a serving dish with the tomatoes and pour about 1 tablespoon of sauce over each eggplant. Sprinkle with the crushed peanuts.

Serve the vegetables with the remaining sauce on the side.

*This is a really tasty and attractive salad that takes just a few minutes to throw together.
The avocado should be ripe enough to form a smooth green paste that holds the salad together
and is contrasted nicely by the sharpness from the vinegar and crunch from the fresh cabbage.*

CABBAGE & ZUCCHINI

Serves 4

Time: 15 minutes

1 zucchini

⅓ green cabbage

1 ripe avocado

½ pound tomatoes

6 sprigs fresh parsley

6 sprigs fresh basil

1 teaspoon ground cumin

1 teaspoon flaky sea salt

1 tablespoon white wine vinegar

1 tablespoon extra virgin olive oil

Finely slice the zucchini and cabbage into long thin slices and place them into a mixing bowl. Halve the avocado and scoop out the flesh. Roughly chop the avocado and mix it in with the zucchini and cabbage with your hands.

Chop the tomatoes, parsley, and basil into small thin slices, then add them to the bowl with the remaining ingredients. Mix well and serve.

Wrapped in old news, suya is the skewered groundnut-, ginger-, and chili-coated grilled meat you'll see vendors nursing on the roadsides. It's served with extra-hot pepper powder and an onion salad, and my father, Chief Brown, stocks up when the kids are in Lagos.

BEEF SUYA

Serves 4

Time: 45 minutes

generous 1 cup roasted peanuts

¾ teaspoon ground ginger

¾ teaspoon ground white pepper

¾ teaspoon cayenne pepper

1 teaspoon onion powder

1 teaspoon garlic powder

5 Grains of Selim/Guinea pepper seeds or 5 black peppercorns and a pinch of nutmeg

½ pound beef (sirloin steak or other steak)

2 tablespoons peanut oil

½ a red onion

a handful of cherry tomatoes

Put the peanuts, ginger, white pepper, cayenne, onion powder, garlic powder, and Grains of Selim into a blender and blend for a few minutes until you have a coarse powder. The peanuts should not be ground too fine, otherwise they will start to form a paste and subsequently turn into peanut butter.

Cut the beef into thin slices. Using a pastry brush, coat the strips of meat liberally with the oil. Spread the peanut mix on a flat surface or plate and dab both surfaces of the meat in the mix until they are well coated.

Load some skewers with pieces of steak, making sure that it is as flat as possible. Sprinkle over the remainder of the peanut mix and leave to rest for 15 minutes at room temperature.

Preheat a broiler or grill and cook the meat for 15 minutes, flipping it every 5 minutes or so. Be sure to pay attention to the meat while grilling, and flip whenever it looks like it is getting too hot.

In the meantime, finely slice the red onion and cut each tomato into small slices. Remove the skewers from the grill, allow to cool to room temperature, and serve with the tomatoes and finely sliced red onion.

*Suya-inspired, we created our own dry rub that easily becomes a marinade
with a little oil, lemon juice, and honey.*

RED RUB

Makes about 5 ounces

Time: 5 minutes

1 tablespoon black peppercorns

1 tablespoon sea salt flakes

4 tablespoons sumac

1 tablespoon dried oregano

½ teaspoon smoked paprika

1 teaspoon granulated
brown sugar

1 tablespoon garlic granules

1 tablespoon onion granules

Coarsely grind the peppercorns with a pestle and mortar.

Add the sea salt flakes and pound for another 30 seconds.

Add all the other ingredients and grind until well integrated.

Store in an airtight container.

I tried with gizzard. That got the thumbs-down and was consigned to the blacklist.

Then I suggested heart, but almost lost heart before I'd even made it. When I finally got around to it we were pleasantly surprised. The sharp marinade cuts the richness of the meat beautifully, but if you're not feeling adventurous it works just as well with lamb shoulder pieces. Make sure you keep the stock after the meat is cooked. It can be used in place of water to make a tasty rice.

GRILLED HEART

Serves 6

Time: 1 hour

4½ tablespoons red rub
(see page 65)

juice of 2 lemons

1 tablespoon honey

2 tablespoons extra virgin olive oil

1 pound chicken hearts or
diced lamb shoulder

Combine 4 tablespoons of the red rub with the lemon juice, honey, and extra virgin olive oil. Add the chicken hearts and leave to marinate for at least half an hour. *The longer you leave them, the deeper the flavor.*

Preheat the broiler to medium-high and broil the hearts in a Pyrex dish (or equivalent) or metal pan with their marinade for 20 minutes.

Remove one of the hearts and cut it in half to check if it's cooked through. If there's some blood and you like your meat well done, return it to the oven for another 5 minutes. If you prefer your meat medium, remove the dish from the oven and leave to stand. It will cook further in the residual heat.

Place a colander over a mixing bowl and drain the liquid from the meat. Sprinkle the remaining ½ tablespoon of red rub over the heart pieces and toss. Serve immediately.

GREEN SALAD WITH TANGERINE DRESSING

Serves 4 (makes about 4 ounces of dressing)

Time: 55 minutes

1 onion

3 tablespoons toasted sesame oil

2 tangerines

¾ inch fresh ginger

½ teaspoon fine sea salt

½ teaspoon coarsely ground black pepper

1 teaspoon dark brown sugar

1 tablespoon white wine vinegar

5 ounces mixed greens (lettuce, watercress, and arugula)

Finely dice the onion and fry with 2 tablespoons of toasted sesame oil in a small pot over low heat. Stir regularly so that the onion becomes sweet and soft without burning. It will take some time for it to caramelize completely.

Zest the tangerines, squeeze 2 tablespoons of the juice, and set aside.

Peel the ginger and crush to a paste using a knife or a fine grater.

In a bowl, mix the cooked onion, tangerine zest and juice, crushed ginger, salt, black pepper, dark brown sugar, white wine vinegar, and the remaining 1 tablespoon of toasted sesame oil.

Wash the greens in cold water and leave them to drain in a colander. Transfer to a serving bowl.

Stir the dressing well and toss with the salad, using roughly 1 teaspoon of dressing for every handful of leaves.

The dressing can be stored in a sealed jar in the fridge for 2 weeks.

Particularly with the nations on the coast of East Africa, there is a long tradition of trade across the Indian Ocean. I've always loved pilau rice, which has a strong connection with Asia, and I ate it regularly while living in Tanzania. I made the pilau I knew for Yemi and Duval. Yemi became very excited about the flavors and possibilities, and set about creating his own. When it came to deciding which to serve at an event, and which for the book, majority ruled, and his, with added hints of lemon, won out. It might not be the most traditional version of a pilau, although it may be one of the most intriguing interpretations of a well-traveled dish.

PILAU

Serves 8

Time: 40 minutes

1⅓ pounds carrots

2 medium onions

2 cloves of garlic

1 ounce fresh turmeric

¼ cup olive oil, plus 1 teaspoon

1 tablespoon cumin seeds

1 teaspoon white peppercorns

2 teaspoons sea salt flakes

2½ cups rice

3 lemons

Peel and coarsely grate the carrots.

Chop the onions, then peel and crush the garlic and fresh turmeric. *It's easiest to do this with a pestle and mortar, but if you don't have one, use the flat side of a knife.*

In a large pot or nonstick saucepan, fry the onions in ¼ cup of oil over medium heat for 3 minutes. Add the carrots and continue frying for another 3 minutes. Add the garlic and turmeric paste and cook for another 4 minutes. The carrots and onions should be soft but retain a little bite.

Crush the cumin seeds and white peppercorns with a pestle and mortar, then add to the carrot base along with the salt. Add the rice, stirring so it is laced with onions, carrots, and seasoning. Pour in 4 cups of boiling water, stir gently, then reduce to a low simmer. Add 1 teaspoon of olive oil, then cover the pot and steam for 8 minutes.

Open the pot and stir the rice gently, ensuring that you get right to the bottom and center of the pan. This helps the rice to cook consistently. Cover and steam for another 8 minutes.

Turn off the heat, but leave covered for 8 minutes more. *Finishing rice with the residual heat improves the taste and texture.*

Take the lid off and fluff up the rice with a fork. Zest the lemons, and stir the zest into the rice just before serving. Serve warm.

BANANA

When I was living in Tanzania bananas were regularly served with pilau rice. They are an ideal accompaniment to flavored rice. We serve them with jollof rice too. They provide a fresh, cooling component to a meal, and work in the place of yogurt, as bananas also take the edge off spicy food. Put them into the fridge to chill them before serving so that they remain firm and cool—even though over the long term this can cause the skin to brown, the interior remains intact. Serve one chilled banana per person with a generous portion of rice.

Growing up all I knew were boiled yam discs, but this recipe transforms the tuber into an exceptional cake. Considering there's no flour it has a beautiful crumb texture. And it's subtly sweet from the little sugar combined with condensed milk, which in turn helps keep the cake surprisingly moist.

For this recipe to work well you'll need a mature puna yam tuber.
They wither with age as the skin and flesh inside dehydrate in tandem.

PUNA YAM CAKE

Makes 1 cake

Time: 1 hour 15 minutes

1 pound fresh puna yam
(peeled weight)

2 small eggs

3½ tablespoons coconut oil
(plus extra for oiling)

¼ cup superfine sugar

¼ teaspoon salt

scant ½ cup condensed milk

½ cup plus 2 tablespoons
coconut milk

generous ½ cup unsweetened
shredded coconut (to garnish)

Preheat the oven to 350°F.

Peel the fresh yam, then finely grate it and set aside. Whisk the eggs, then set aside. Melt the coconut oil (if solid). Add the sugar to the oil and whisk well together. Combine all the ingredients (except for the shredded coconut) and mix well.

Thoroughly oil a 1-pound loaf pan or a 9-inch round cake pan. Add the mixture and then bake on the middle rack for 1 hour.

Leave the cake to cool, then garnish it with the shredded coconut.

This tea is incredibly refreshing and comforting at the same time.
It's perfect after a meal or with a slice of cake.

MINT TEA

Bring 1 quart of water to a simmer in a small pan. Roughly rip up a bunch of fresh mint, add it to the pan, and stir well for 30 seconds. Leave the tea to simmer over medium heat for 10 minutes. It is important that there is time for the mint to impart its flavor. Strain through a fine sieve into a pitcher. Serve hot in small glasses, with optional sugar.

menu

"The soup did not and does not disappoint—reviews still flood in every time we make it."

I'd heard so much about this fabled green soup that Yemi had created following a trip with Duval. It was intended as the centerpiece to the menu, and it stood confidently as the first dish of our third event. We added soup bowls to our repertoire for the occasion and served it with steamed buns. The soup did not and does not disappoint—reviews still flood in every time we make it.

Menu discussion continued. We talked about hard fish. Not dried fish. Nor dry. Nor, really, hard. It had to be like the barracuda that Duval's grandma made; like the fish they serve at Bola's and other takeout spots around London. It had a lot to live up to. With the imagined final dish in mind, kingfish was the solution. It triumphed during our cooking trials, standing strong while others flaked and fell apart.

The other elements developed naturally and were intentionally on the light side, taking dessert into

consideration. The fennel and tomato complemented the fish as a cooked salad, and the red cabbage dish had been a candidate for the first menu. The coconut and spices are typical of the East coast, and millet is produced and popular in many African countries. Apples picked at his grandparents' house inspired Duval's sauce. And we also made a late addition that relied heavily on choosing the right ingredients from the market, trusting each other over the phone.

Can you pick up some plantain in the morning? *Which ones?* Green green for the crisps. Yellowy black to steam. *I'll have a look. Ripe?* Yeah, not soft though! And don't forget the green. Super green for the crisps. *How many?* Like ten to fifteen green, twenty ripe ones. We've still got some left from yesterday, no? *Yeah, yeah.* Cool. And get some bananas while you're at it, please. Ripe ones, yeah? They need to be sweet. *Yep.* Nice one.

I started making my own ginger beer years ago as an ongoing artwork.
I was taught the traditional West African recipe by my grandma, which I decanted
into flat, circular glass bottles and sold on the street with friends.

Over the years, this recipe has evolved and been fine-tuned through dinner parties, gifts, carnivals, picnics, and Groundnut dinners. The sliced fresh ginger offers a powerful kick of healthy spice without bitterness, the cloves give warmth and depth, the lime juice is sharp and bright, and using golden syrup instead of sugar offers a smooth texture and round flavor that binds the drink together.

GINGER BEER

Makes 3 quarts

Time: 1 hour 20 minutes

1 pound fresh ginger

15 cloves

3½ quarts water

4 limes

generous ¾ cup golden syrup

Peel the ginger. *Using a spoon to scrape away the skin rather than a peeler or knife allows you to navigate in and around awkward areas of the ginger and reduce waste.* Cut the ginger into 1/16-inch-thick slices.

Put the ginger, cloves, and water into a large pot. Bring to a boil, then reduce the heat to medium-low and simmer for 1 hour.

While the ginger is cooking, halve the limes, squeeze their juice, and put to one side. Discard the skins.

Remove the pot from the heat and strain the liquid through a sieve into another large pan to remove the ginger and cloves. While it is still hot, add the golden syrup and stir well. Leave to cool to room temperature.

Add the lime juice and stir well. Strain the mixture through cheesecloth or a fine sieve and decant into sterilized bottles.

Refrigerate the ginger beer and serve chilled over ice.

STEAMED BUNS

Makes 8–12 small buns

Time: 40 minutes (plus 2 hours resting)

1 teaspoon active dry yeast

1 teaspoon carob molasses (or alternative molasses/ golden syrup/honey)

1¾ cups all-purpose flour

2 tablespoons cornstarch

1 teaspoon ground allspice

1 teaspoon ground cinnamon

1 teaspoon ground ginger

1 teaspoon light brown sugar

1 teaspoon fine table salt

1 teaspoon pure vanilla extract

1 teaspoon sea salt flakes, for sprinkling

Whisk together the yeast, molasses, and ½ cup of warm water and leave for 15 minutes.

In a large bowl, sift together the flour, cornstarch, allspice, cinnamon, and ginger. Stir in the sugar and table salt and mix together.

Add the yeast mixture and vanilla to the flour mixture and stir with a fork until it stiffens. Once it's a solid ball, transfer to a floured surface and knead for 5–10 minutes, until it becomes a dough that is soft to the touch but not moist. It should bounce back slightly when a finger is pressed gently on the surface.

Roll into small table-tennis size balls and place on a floured surface. Cover and leave for at least 2 hours in a warm place.

Bring water under a steamer to a boil. *Make sure that it is not boiling too vigorously, otherwise the water might splash the buns.* Reduce to a simmer.

Lightly oil the steamer insert by applying oil to a paper towel and wiping it across the insert, or place a small round of lightly oiled parchment paper on the bottom of the steamer insert to prevent the buns from sticking. Place the buns in the steamer, leaving a little room for expansion. Cook for 25 minutes, until the buns are soft to the touch but bounce back once depressed with a finger.

Remove and place on paper towels. Sprinkle with the sea salt while still moist, so it sticks to the surface.

Serve at room temperature, or reheat in the oven at 350°F for 5 minutes.

It sounds like a dream, but I first tasted this soup in a tree house restaurant looking over the Atlantic. I was flying high in Tobago with Duval, and our friends Ininaa and Ibiye, where we made memories for a lifetime.

Ininaa and Ibs proposed that we check out a waterfall on the other side of the island, with a restaurant nearby, and we were down. It was a slow journey, meandering round roads that cut through the greenery. But the waterfall was definitely worth it, like nothing else I had seen for real. We busied ourselves climbing, diving, and chilling and as we simmered down it was about that time. Time for this mystery tree house restaurant, which Ininaa warned was a bit special. I was beyond hungry.

The first thing to arrive was a deep green callaloo soup. In truth, I don't remember the rest of the meal because this completely took over. I readied myself with spoon in hand and was shaking a little. My tastebuds were already alive and when the spoon delivered it didn't disappoint. Nothing has ever tasted that good.

I returned home in search of the dragon, researching and testing different recipes, and my favorite components from each formed my own new creation.

GREEN SOUP

Serves 15

Time: 45 minutes

3 green bananas

19-ounce can of callaloo

¼ pound okra

1 yellow bell pepper

1 Scotch bonnet pepper, seeded

3 onions

4 cloves of garlic

3 celery stalks (with leaves)

1 pound spinach

1 quart vegetable stock (see page 313)

1⅔ cups coconut milk

1 teaspoon dried thyme

2 teaspoons sea salt flakes

1 teaspoon coarsely ground black pepper

Top and tail the green bananas, then make a skin-deep incision in the skin from top to the bottom on both sides. Peel.

Drain the canned callaloo, but do not rinse.

Roughly wash and chop the rest of the vegetables, paying particular attention to washing the spinach.

Put the bananas, callaloo, and the other vegetables (except the spinach, which you'll add later) into a very large deep saucepan. Add the stock, coconut milk, and thyme and stir well. Bring the mixture to a boil, cover, and cook over medium heat for 25 minutes. *The surface of the soup should be bubbling gently throughout.*

Add the spinach, stir well until wilted, and cook for another 5 minutes. *Adding the spinach later ensures that the soup is a vivid green color.*

Remove from the heat and blend the soup until smooth, using a stick blender. Season with the salt and coarse black pepper. Taste and season further if you see fit.

This is a beautiful cooked salad that goes really well with fish and meat dishes.
The ingredients fit together wonderfully.

FENNEL & TOMATO

Serves 4

Time: 35 minutes

2 fennel bulbs (ideally, pick
small, fresh-looking, firm
and unblemished bulbs)

3 tablespoons olive oil

a pinch of sea salt flakes

7 ounces cherry tomatoes
(on the vine if possible)

1 tablespoon balsamic vinegar

a pinch of finely ground
black pepper

Preheat the oven to 390°F.

Cut off and discard the hard base of the fennel. Trim and chop the small leaves and foliage and set aside. If the fennel is particularly fibrous-looking—*showing prominent green strips*—use a vegetable peeler to lift the base of each fiber at the tip and pull them out.

Cut each fennel bulb in half. Place the halves flat on a work surface and slice each one into 4–5 pieces lengthwise. Arrange on a baking sheet, ensuring that each piece has a little room to breathe. Sprinkle with the olive oil and sea salt and mix well so that the fennel is evenly coated.

Put the baking sheet into the oven for 15 minutes, then remove and add the cherry tomatoes, still on the vine. Drizzle with the balsamic vinegar and bake for another 10–15 minutes, or until the tomatoes have just softened but still hold their shape.

Sprinkle with the black pepper and reserved chopped fennel leaves, and serve hot or cold.

RED CABBAGE & COCONUT

Serves 4

Time: 1 hour 5 minutes

1 tablespoon coconut oil

2 onions, diced

1 long green chili, seeded and finely chopped

1 ounce fresh ginger, peeled and finely chopped

2 cloves of garlic, sliced

1 teaspoon ground coriander

1 teaspoon pan-roasted and crushed cumin seeds, or ground cumin

1 teaspoon sea salt flakes

½ teaspoon black pepper

1 small red cabbage

2 ounces creamed coconut

1½–1⅔ cups hot vegetable stock (see page 313)

Heat the coconut oil over medium-low heat. Add the onions and fry for 5 minutes, or until slightly softened. Add the chili, ginger, garlic, coriander, cumin, salt, and pepper and fry for another 10 minutes.

Meanwhile, cut the red cabbage into thick dice (the cabbage cooks more quickly the smaller it is cut) and set aside. Grate the creamed coconut into a bowl and set aside.

When the onions have cooked for about 15 minutes and are browned, add the cabbage, turn the heat up slightly and cook, stirring regularly, for 5 minutes.

Reduce the heat to low and add the grated creamed coconut. Mix well and cook for 2 minutes, then gradually stir in the stock.

Leave over low heat for 15–20 minutes, then stir and serve.

This humble way to prepare plantain is probably my favorite. The steaming process develops the complex natural sweetness, and below we've given three ways to achieve the same warm and comforting outcome.

STEAMED PLANTAIN

Serves 4

Time: 10 minutes

4 yellow-black plantains

To steam

Rinse the plantains and scrub well. Top and tail, then make a skin-deep incision and peel. Boil water in a pot and lightly oil the bottom of a steamer insert. This prevents the plantains from sticking to the surface. Steam for 15 minutes with the lid on. To check if they're done, remove one piece and halve crosswise. If the outer yellow color is consistent throughout, it's ready.

To bake

Preheat the oven to 350°F.

Rinse the plantains and scrub well. Top and tail them, then make a skin-deep incision from top to bottom. Do not peel.

Wrap loosely in foil and bake whole in their skins for 25 minutes.

To microwave

Prepare the plantains as if baking, but do not wrap in foil. Place them one at a time on a microwavable plate. Cover and microwave on the highest setting for 2½ minutes.

Leave to stand in the microwave for 2 minutes.

My grandparents have always been into gardening. As children we ran around spotting fruits and vegetables hanging among the beautiful leaves and flowers that circled the walled garden—plums, runner beans, tomatoes, zucchini, and rhubarb. In October I had bags overflowing with tasty apples from the small trees just by their front door. I decided to chop up a handful of them and throw them into the oven with some Scotch bonnet pepper, fennel seeds, and a chicken I was roasting at the time. Something magical happened and the sweet, spicy sauce that came out was truly special.

ROASTED APPLE & SCOTCH BONNET SAUCE

Makes 1¼ cups sauce

Time: 1 hour 10 minutes

1⅓ pounds apples (about 5)

½ a Scotch bonnet pepper

1 teaspoon coarse crystal salt

1 teaspoon fennel seeds

1 tablespoon olive oil

Preheat the oven to 395°F.

Wash and core the apples, then cut them into 1½-inch chunks and put them into a Dutch oven or roasting pan. Use a pan small enough that the apples are heaped on top of each other. *This will encourage a sauce to form while cooking.*

Seed the Scotch bonnet pepper and dice it as finely as possible. *The smaller the pieces, the more evenly the heat will be distributed through the sauce.* Wear gloves when chopping the pepper to protect yourself.

Crush the salt and fennel seeds with a pestle and mortar.

Add the Scotch bonnet and the seed mixture to the apples and mix well. Cover with foil and cook in the middle of the oven for 45–60 minutes, or until the apples break down, soften, and turn into a sauce.

When the apples have dissolved into a very soft sauce that is beginning to brown in places, remove them from the oven.

Serve in a small bowl.

Millet is a small grain, indigenous to West Africa, that grows across the continent in hot and dry regions, where it is used as a staple like rice or couscous. There are loads of varieties of millet, including pearl millet, finger millet, and fonio, that vary in size and color. A variety with a large grain such as pearl millet works well for this recipe. The gluten-free seeds are an easy ingredient to cook with because they can absorb a lot of water without becoming soggy, so they are very forgiving if you add too much water or stock. You can find millet in African and Asian shops as well as at many natural foods stores and online retailers.

MILLET

Serves 4

Time: 15 minutes

14 ounces steamed and dried pearl millet balls

3 cups hot vegetable stock (see page 313)

Dry-fry the millet balls in a wide pan for 2 minutes over medium heat, stirring regularly.

Once the millet balls have browned nicely, add the hot stock to the pan and cook over medium heat for 10 minutes, stirring occasionally.

Once the millet has absorbed the stock, taste it—it should be soft but still maintain some bite. If the millet is crunchy, add small amounts of stock or water and leave it over low heat until it is cooked.

Serve hot or cold.

We sought out fishmongers, looking for a fish with adequate body to produce the hard fish dish we had discussed and all imagined vividly—firm, crispy, flavorful, and a delight to eat. After cooking trials, kingfish, a large powerful fish, prospered. A cross section of it forms a nice portion that holds up well to cooking. It has no tiny bones and a prominent central spine, which is satisfyingly bare once all the juicy flesh has been picked off it.

Deep-frying kingfish is where you really get the texture we seek. A crisp skin flecked with ginger, garlic, and sea salt flakes concealing a moist but firm flesh. Ideally we serve it fresh before it has time to cool down, with a dash of lemon, although cool kingfish is another treat altogether. A great addition to a picnic, perhaps. This fish also holds up well to broiling, pan-frying, and grilling.

KINGFISH

Serves 4

**Time: 18 minutes
(plus 2 hours marinating)**

1 ounce fresh ginger

2 cloves of garlic

1 teaspoon salt

4 kingfish steaks, approx. ¾ inch
thick (cut crosswise)

2 quarts plus 1 teaspoon
sunflower oil

4 lemon wedges, to serve

Peel and finely dice the ginger and garlic, then crush with a knife, with a pestle and mortar, or in a blender, using the salt to help the process.

Mix the garlic and ginger with the kingfish and add 1 teaspoon of sunflower oil. Place the fish in a ceramic or glass dish, cover with plastic wrap, and leave to marinate in the fridge for 2 hours.

Remove the fish from the fridge half an hour before cooking and heat 2 quarts of sunflower oil to 375°F. *It's helpful to have a thermometer to measure the temperature. If you don't have a thermometer, heat the oil until a small cube of bread placed in the oil turns golden brown in 30 seconds—when it does, your oil is hot enough to deep-fry.*

Once the oil is at the correct temperature, gently drop in the fish steaks and fry for 5–8 minutes, depending on size. Remove the fish with a slotted spoon when just starting to brown—the fish darkens further once removed from the oil—and drain on paper towels. Serve hot with lemon wedges.

Leave the oil to cool, then store in a sealed container. It can be used again (but only for fishy things) and will keep for a long time.

We generally don't like cakes to be too sweet. In this recipe a lot of the sweetness comes from the banana, and it is wheat- and lactose-free. We have often discussed our fondness for no-fuss standard pound cakes. Accordingly, this recipe is for a quick, simple banana loaf cake that you might accompany with a hot drink.

BANANA ALMOND CAKE

Makes one 2-pound loaf

Time: 1 hour

1 teaspoon sunflower oil

3 medium eggs, lightly beaten

3 ripe (or overripe) bananas, mashed

6 tablespoons superfine sugar

generous 2¾ cups ground almonds

1 teaspoon baking powder

Heat the oven to 350°F. Grease a 2-pound loaf pan with oil or butter and line with parchment paper.

Put the eggs, mashed bananas, and sugar into a bowl and beat lightly.

Mix the ground almonds with the baking powder, then fold into the egg mixture until well combined.

Pour the batter into the lined pan and level the surface with a spatula.

Put into the oven for 25 minutes. Insert a metal skewer or toothpick into the middle, and if it comes out clean, the cake is ready.

Allow to cool (this cake is not at its best hot, as the flavors appear to settle as it cools).

Cut into thick slices to serve.

This recipe owes a debt to Rose Bakery in Paris, where I first started to make ginger cake.

GINGER CAKE

Makes one 2-pound cake

Time: 45 minutes

¾ cup plus 2 tablespoons all-purpose flour

¾ cup plus 2 tablespoons whole wheat flour

1 teaspoon baking powder

1 teaspoon ground cinnamon

½ teaspoon ground allspice

a pinch of cayenne pepper

2 tablespoons ground ginger

a pinch of salt

1 teaspoon baking soda

5 tablespoons unsalted butter, softened

1 tablespoon muscovado sugar

3 tablespoons golden syrup, plus extra to serve

2 tablespoons molasses

2 ounces fresh ginger, peeled, grated, and crushed to a paste

¾ cup evaporated milk

2 eggs, beaten

Preheat the oven to 350°F and grease a 2-pound loaf pan.

Put the flours, baking powder, cinnamon, allspice, cayenne, ground ginger, salt, and baking soda into a bowl and mix together.

In a separate bowl, beat together the softened butter, muscovado sugar, golden syrup, molasses, fresh ginger paste, and evaporated milk until well combined.

Add the dry ingredients to the bowl of wet ingredients and beat well, until a consistent paste is formed. Mix in the beaten eggs in roughly three additions, beating after each one.

Pour the mixture into the greased loaf pan. Holding the ends of the pan, tap it firmly on a hard surface to level the mixture and get rid of air bubbles. Place in the preheated oven for 30 minutes, or until you can stick a metal skewer or toothpick in the middle and it comes out clean.

Once the cake is ready, take it out of the oven and allow to cool before delicately sliding a knife between the edge of the pan and the cake. Remove from the pan and serve in slices. It is also lovely drizzled with a bit more golden syrup.

menu

"Noodles. We wanted to serve them the way we've seen them in so many American movies. Gobbled up out of steaming white paper boxes with chopsticks."

Toward the end of summer, we met on a quiet patch of grass by a pond in Hyde Park to discuss ideas for our next menu while catching the last of the evening sunshine. Jacob had just returned from working and visiting family in Kenya, South Sudan, and Burundi, Yemi had been to a music festival in the South of France and I'd been on a trip to Amsterdam. The meeting was a great one and we all shared the desire to create something new.

Noodles. We wanted to serve them the way we've seen them in so many American movies. Gobbled up out of steaming white paper boxes with chopsticks. A few days later, Jacob and I visited a friend who is an expert on udon noodles to ask for

some advice. He offered to let us use his renowned noodles, just so long as we "Don't f*** it up!" We left honored, excited, and a bit scared. Although it was great to receive the offer, the main thing we drew was inspiration to create our very own cornmeal noodles.

The rest of the menu took shape around our noodles, with a combination of rich flavors from the pork in tamarind and the stewed plums juxtaposed with the freshness of the cucumber and chile drink, the pea soup, and the fresh tarragon from the avocado ice cream. This is one of our favorite and most original menus because of the variety of ingredients and how well they work together.

A year without Carnival is like one without a birthday.
It's a measure of our days and an unspoken fixture in the calendar.

It all starts south of the river. Then we roll westward together, all laughs and smiles.
Electric uniforms and unfamiliar faces greet us on the underground. Then we stop for a
moment to take it all in.

Being a tall man, I'm a signpost for anybody who's lost. And in the spirit
of losing yourself, you'll always find one of us at Channel One sound system,
swaying to deep dub, and probably drinking from the bottle.

CARNIVAL COCKTAIL

Makes 1 quart
Time: 10 minutes

2 cucumbers

2½ ounces fresh lime juice

2 tablespoons chopped fresh mint

½ medium-hot green chile

3 tablespoons superfine sugar

2½ ounces water

3½ ounces overproof white rum

2½ ounces golden tequila

sprigs of mint, to serve

Peel and slice the cucumbers. Squeeze the lime juice, pick and chop the mint leaves, and seed the chile.

Put all the ingredients (except for the rum and tequila) into a blender and whizz until smooth. You could serve it now if you're not a drinker.

Add rum and tequila to taste. Serve over plenty of ice, with sprigs of mint.

I insisted that an aunt teach me how to make samosas in Nakuru, Kenya, after once seeing her make them and serve them to the family. It was the gardener, Justin, who showed her how it was done, and one afternoon the opportunity arose to have a lesson from the master pastry chef/ gardener. Justin meticulously schooled me—from making the dough to removing the samosas from the deep-fryer. I scribbled instructions, quantities, timings, and even schematic drawings on paper with the verve of an eager student.

Samosa cases are an incredible thing to make. So simple—flour, water, salt, and sugar— yet the process (which is not so straightforward) is remarkable. One stage in particular, when the samosa shells peel off leaflike, is like a magic trick.

NAKURU SAMOSA SHELLS WITH KIDNEY BEANS IN COCONUT

Makes 16 samosas

Time: 1 hour (plus 3 minutes per samosa)

1 cup plus 6 tablespoons all-purpose flour

½ teaspoon sugar

½ teaspoon salt

7 tablespoons warm water

peanut or vegetable oil, for brushing

For the filling

4 medium onions

2 cloves of garlic

2 teaspoons salt

2 tablespoons extra virgin coconut oil

1 teaspoon creamed coconut

scant ½ cup vegetable stock (see page 313)

½ teaspoon dried thyme

1 teaspoon freshly ground black pepper

4½ cups cooked kidney beans

2 quarts peanut or vegetable oil, for deep-frying

Place 1 cup plus 3 tablespoons of flour, the sugar, and salt into a bowl and add the warm water slowly, mixing with a fork until it forms a stiff paste. With your hands, knead the dough until it is in a solid dry ball that is slightly sticky to the touch, then separate it into 4 table-tennis-size balls.

Roll the balls into small discs (5 inch diameter), about ⅛ inch thick. Ensure that they are of equal size. On a floured surface, take one of the discs and generously brush a layer of oil on the top with a pastry brush. Repeat with the remaining three and stack on top of each other, with a layer of oil separating them.

Press a finger in around the edge of each stack of dough about eight times. Then turn over the dough with the finger depressions underneath and gently run a rolling pin over it in a circular motion. Flatten and flip the dough repeatedly until it is roughly crêpe size and ⅛ inch thick (12 inch diameter). Cut around the edges of the flattened dough with a knife to make it perfectly round, and remove any dough that remains visibly layered. Quarter the dough by drawing a straight cross with a sharp knife from edge to edge. Heat a hot flat metal pan to a medium heat and add ½ teaspoon of oil. Lay one of the triangular quarters of dough on the hot pan for 1 minute, then flip the triangle with a spatula. Peel off the top layer, which should naturally start to separate, and put to one side. Continue this process, lightly frying the layers until they peel off. Set aside.

In a cup, mix the remaining 3 tablespoons of flour with 3–4 tablespoons of cold water until it has a thick, smooth, gluey consistency.

With the triangle pointing towards you like an arrow, fold the top right-hand corner across until it reaches approximately one-third of the way across the opposite corner. Fold the top left-hand corner across so that only the tip of the arrow appears to be facing you. Add a thin layer of flour/water glue mix to bind the overlapping triangle.

Once all the shells have been made, begin making the filling. Peel and finely slice the onions and peel and crush the garlic to a paste with ½ teaspoon of salt. In a large frying pan, fry the onions in the coconut oil over high heat for 10 minutes, stirring attentively as they brown. Add the garlic and fry for another 5 minutes.

In the same pan, dissolve the creamed coconut in the stock, then add the thyme, pepper, and remaining 1½ teaspoons of salt. Rinse and drain the kidney beans, then add to the pan. Heat gently for 5 minutes, then mash roughly. Allow to cool for 10 minutes.

Fill the samosa shells with the kidney bean mixture and fold down the other corner so a small package is made. Set aside and allow the flour paste to set. Heat the oil to 350°F and fry the samosas in batches for 3 minutes, until they start to brown slightly. Serve hot or cold.

When this bread is fresh from the oven I like to eat it on its own, otherwise it is a great accompaniment to a soup or salad and makes a crunchy aromatic toast.

TEA BREAD

Makes one large loaf

Time: 1 hour 25 minutes (plus 1 hour 30 minutes for bread to rise)

butter (for greasing)

2 unwaxed lemons

4 cups bread flour

1 tablespoon active dry yeast

scant ½ ounce rooibos tea (about 4 tea bags)

½ teaspoon table salt

2 tablespoons golden syrup

1 cup warm water

1 teaspoon sea salt flakes

Butter a rimmed baking sheet, cake pan, or Dutch oven.

Strip the zest off both lemons, using a vegetable peeler, and slice the zest into long thin strips 1/16 inch wide. Slice off the white pith of the lemon and discard, then chop the flesh into small chunks and remove the seeds.

Put 3¼ cups of flour into a large bowl with the yeast, tea leaves, table salt, lemon zest, and flesh. Mix well to distribute the yeast throughout, then add the golden syrup.

Add the water to the bowl while stirring and mix well until the mixture forms a wet dough.

Put the remaining ¾ cup of flour on a clean surface and put the dough on top of it. With floured hands, begin to knead the mixture into a firmer dough by folding the edge of the mixture into the middle, pushing down and rotating it 90°, and repeating. Knead the dough for 12 minutes. Keep the surface and your hands well floured.

Shape the bread how you like, with or without a pan. Keep in mind that the bread will rise considerably. Sprinkle the sea salt flakes over the surface of the dough and gently push the salt into the surface to create a tasty salty crust. Place the dough on the greased baking sheet, cake pan, or Dutch oven, cover with a clean tea towel and leave in a warm place to rise for 90 minutes.

Preheat the oven to 395°F.

Half-fill a shallow roasting pan with boiling water and place at the bottom of the oven. *This will add steam to the oven, which helps to keep the skin of the dough moist, therefore allowing it to expand.* Put the bread in the middle of the oven. After 15 minutes, turn down the heat to 350°F and cook for 10–15 minutes more.

Take the bread out of the oven and leave to cool slightly. If the base of the bread is moist, remove it from the pan, turn it over, and put it back into the oven for another 5–10 minutes. When the crust of the bread is golden and the loaf sounds hollow when you tap it from underneath, it is ready.

Serve warm or at room temperature. Once the bread has cooled completely, it can be stored in an airtight place or wrapped with plastic wrap to keep it fresh for up to 2 days.

One for summer.

PEA SOUP

Serves 4

Time: 35 minutes

2 green bananas

½ a leek

6 small scallions

1 green chile, seeded

1 clove of garlic, crushed

5 cups hot vegetable stock
(see page 313)

14 ounces frozen petits pois

2 tablespoons fresh lime juice

¼ teaspoon superfine sugar

3 tablespoons chopped fresh mint

Peel the green bananas, then roughly chop with the leek, scallions, and green chile. Put into a large deep-sided pan with the garlic and add the hot stock.

Bring to a boil, then simmer over low heat, covered with a lid, for 20 minutes.

Add half the petits pois, simmer for a final 2 minutes, then remove from the heat. Add the lime juice, sugar, and mint, and blend thoroughly.

Add the remaining petits pois but leave them whole. This adds some bite to the soup.

Allow to cool, and refrigerate until ready to serve. Serve chilled.

This recipe takes time and effort—however, once you start to get a feel for making these, the process should become very manageable and fun to do. Crafted by your own hands, these rustic noodles can be served in white paper noodle boxes with chopsticks.

CORNMEAL NOODLES

Serves 6

**Time: 1 hour 15 minutes
(plus 4 hours resting time)**

1¼ cups white cornmeal

2 teaspoons salt

2¾ cups all-purpose flour
(plus extra for rolling)

1 tablespoon olive oil

Put the cornmeal and salt into a pan with 4 cups of cold water and cook over medium-low heat for 30 minutes, firmly stirring every few minutes with a strong wooden spoon. After 30 minutes, the cornmeal will have absorbed the water and become a soft white dough. Taste it—once it has become quite solid and the texture is smooth and not grainy, take the pan off the heat.

Put 2 cups of the flour into a large bowl. Put the cornmeal dough into the middle of the flour and mix it with a wooden spoon for a couple of minutes, until all the flour has combined with the cornmeal to form a tough dough. Leave to cool for a few minutes.

On a well-floured surface, knead the dough for 10 minutes, making sure your hands are also well floured. Shape it into a flat block roughly 2 inches thick, wrap in plastic wrap, and place in the fridge for 4 hours.

Sprinkle the remaining ¾ cup flour on a clean, dry surface and place the dough on top. Knead it for 5 minutes, until you are able to stretch it slightly without it breaking. Meanwhile, bring 4 quarts of water to a boil in a large pan.

On a floured surface, roll the dough out into a rough square or rectangle ⅛ inch thick. Make sure both sides of the dough are lightly floured. Take the side of the dough the furthest away from your body and fold it over to meet the side closest to you. Don't press down.

With a long, sharp knife, cut the dough into ⅓-inch-wide vertical slices. Unfold each slice and delicately dust off any excess flour, then drop the noodles into the boiling water one at a time.

After 3 minutes, when the noodles float to the top, remove them from the water with a wide draining spoon and place them in a colander. Rinse them under cold water for 5 seconds. Any flour residue can be removed from the noodles by running your hands gently along the surface. Drain the noodles in the colander, then put them into a bowl.

Serve hot or cold.

I started experimenting with poultry in broth after being served poached chicken by a Ugandan friend, Matthius, who I studied with. It is a great, simple, and tasty way to cook poultry. This recipe makes delicious chicken, and the by-product is a tasty broth that can be eaten alongside or on its own. Taking the meat off the bone and tossing it with fresh vegetables adds a delightful freshness and crunchiness to the dish.

POACHED CHICKEN

Serves 4

Time: 1 hour 5 minutes

about ¼ pound fresh ginger

1 whole chicken (about 2½ pounds), skinned

3 star anise

2 tablespoons fennel seeds

3 tablespoons plum brandy or another sweet brandy

3 tablespoons light brown sugar

1 teaspoon black peppercorns

2 tablespoons fenugreek seeds

5 tablespoons light soy sauce

1 teaspoon salt

2 scallions

To serve

6 scallions

2 carrots

¼ cup creamed coconut

Peel and roughly slice the ginger. Put all the ingredients into a pan that the chicken can easily fit into, and add water until the chicken is covered. Bring to a boil, then turn down to a simmer for about 35–45 minutes.

Finely chop the 6 scallions and carrots and grate the creamed coconut and set aside.

Take the chicken out of the liquid, and set the liquid aside. Once it has cooled slightly, remove the chicken from the bone and put it into a bowl.

Toss the chicken while still warm with the scallions, carrots, and creamed coconut. Pour a few tablespoons of the cooking liquid over the chicken so that it is moist but not wet. Serve hot.

Once you have taken the chicken out of the cooking liquid, put the pan back over a medium-high heat and bubble for another hour. *This will concentrate the flavor of the stock.* You can use this as a broth for a soup or as a base for another sauce.

Tamarind is usually sold in three forms: pods, blocks, and concentrate. I strongly suggest that you use the concentrate for this marinade. It's much easier to use than pods and blocks, and keeps for a long time. If you do have fresh tamarind pods, crack the shells and remove the case and the fibrous veins that surround the sticky pulp. Refrigerating makes them easy to peel. You can use pork loin chops for this recipe, but shoulder is better because of the marbles of fat that run through it. This tamarind marinade can also be used to coat cubed butternut squash before roasting it until sticky and caramelized.

PORK IN TAMARIND

Serves 6

**Time: 50 minutes
(plus 2 hours marinating)**

1¾ pounds pork shoulder chops

6 scallions

2 large carrots

**For the marinade
(makes about 1⅔ cups)**

¼ cup tamarind concentrate

5 tablespoons honey

1 pound fresh blueberries, mashed

2 tablespoons garlic granules

2 tablespoons salt

1 tablespoon smoked paprika

1 tablespoon sumac

1 tablespoon coarse black pepper

1 tablespoon extra virgin olive oil

1 tablespoon balsamic vinegar

Put all the marinade ingredients into a large bowl and stir well. Add the chops and cover with the marinade. Refrigerate for 2 hours.

Preheat the oven to 395°F. Place the pork on a rimmed baking sheet. Roast the pork on the middle rack for 30 minutes, then turn the broiler to medium.

Remove the meat from the oven and slice it into long ⅓-inch-wide strips. Return them to the baking sheet with their juices, and finish under the broiler for a final 10 minutes. *The marinade will concentrate and become even darker and stickier.*

While the meat is broiling, finely slice the scallions and finely grate the carrots. Garnish the pork and serve with noodles.

This is a very wholesome and attractive salad with a rich flavor and a nice amount of crunch. You will be left with extra pesto, which can be stored and used as a spread, a sauce, or simply to make this salad quickly on another occasion.

SPINACH & GREEN BEAN SALAD WITH PEANUT PESTO

Serves 4
(makes 1¼ cups of pesto)
Time: 50 minutes

3 ounces raw red-skinned peanuts

½ a clove of garlic

14 ounces spinach

1 teaspoon table salt, plus a pinch

a wedge of lime

⅔ cup extra virgin olive oil

10 ounces green beans

Preheat the oven to 395°F.

Place the peanuts on a baking sheet and bake in the oven for 10 minutes, shaking the pan once after 5 minutes. When the peanuts are browned and beginning to crack, remove them from the oven and leave to cool.

Crush the garlic to a fine paste with a knife or with a mortar and pestle.

Wash the spinach, then place half of it in a blender with the 1 teaspoon salt, crushed garlic, a squeeze of lime juice, and half the peanuts. Gradually add the oil a little at a time and blend until the mixture forms a pesto with a rough, crunchy texture and all the oil has been added. The pesto can be kept in a jar in the fridge for a week.

Bring a small pan of water to a boil with a pinch of salt. Prepare a bowl of cold water with ice.

Wash, top and tail the green beans, then boil for 2 minutes. Drain the beans and put into the bowl of iced water for 2 minutes, then drain again. With a sharp knife, slice in half lengthwise so that the inner beans are revealed. Put to one side.

Holding the rest of the spinach in a tight bunch, cut across the leaves to form ⅛-inch-wide slices. Start at the top of the spinach leaves and work your way down the stems, discarding the base.

In a large bowl, mix the sliced green beans and spinach. Add 2 tablespoons of peanut and spinach pesto and toss well. Roughly chop the remaining peanuts and sprinkle over the salad.

GROUNDNUT & ALMOND ICE CREAM

Makes 3 cups

Time: 55 minutes

9 ounces unsalted peanuts, with skins

9 ounces almonds, with skins

1 teaspoon salt

1⅔ cups coconut milk

2 tablespoons brown sugar

leaves from 15 sprigs of fresh thyme

Preheat the oven to 395°F.

Put the peanuts, almonds, and salt on a rimmed baking sheet and place in the oven for 12 minutes, until they are golden brown and crunchy. Shake the pan occasionally to ensure that the nuts roast evenly.

Put three-quarters of the roasted nuts into a blender and blend until they form a smooth butter. This process will take around 30 minutes. Give the blender a break every 5 minutes to ensure it doesn't overheat. Once you have a smooth mixture with a runny consistency, add the coconut milk, sugar, fresh thyme leaves, and the remaining nuts and pulse for 30 seconds.

Pour the mixture into a freezerproof container and place in the freezer for at least 5 hours. Use an ice cream scoop to scoop out balls of the ice cream, and serve.

Avocado is naturally smooth, creamy, and rich, so it produces an indulgent ice cream. Any variety of avocado will work, but look out for large green ones with smooth, thin skin and use them when they are slightly soft.

AVOCADO & TARRAGON ICE CREAM

Serves 4

Time: 8 minutes (plus 6 hours freezing time)

2 large avocados

2 lemons

1⅓ cups light brown sugar

15 fresh tarragon leaves

a pinch of salt

Halve the avocados and remove the pits. If there is any residue of flesh around the pits, scrape it off with a spoon. Scoop out all the flesh from the avocado skins and roughly chop.

Halve the lemons and squeeze the juice, removing any seeds.

Blend all the ingredients until you have a silky-smooth green paste. Put the mixture into a freezerproof container and cover. Put into the freezer for at least 4 hours, then remove and scoop out balls with an ice cream scoop.

Serve immediately.

When I was growing up in Tanzania my mother often used to cook stewed plums, which I loved. I suggested that we serve this as a dessert at one of our events. In putting it together, a friend—Julie—suggested that we add something crunchy, and, after a little experimentation, we settled on a crumble topping. We united the plums and loose crumble with the avocado and tarragon ice cream on page 137. The outcome was fantastic—hot sweet plums, cold soothing ice cream, and as much buttery, sugary, and nutty crunch as you'd like to sprinkle on.

STEWED PLUMS & LOOSE CRUMBLE

Serves 4 (with leftover crumble)

Time: 1 hour 30 minutes

7 ounces whole almonds

½ cup demerara sugar

1⅔ cups whole wheat flour

4 ounces salted butter, softened

12 plums

¼ cup granulated sugar

Preheat the oven to 350°F.

Put the almonds on a cutting board and either cover them with a clean tea towel, then beat with a rolling pin to crush them, or chop them with a knife. Alternatively you can use a food processor. Set aside.

Put the demerara sugar, flour, and butter into a bowl and mix well with your hands until the flour has a rough consistency. Add the almonds and spread the mix evenly on a baking sheet large enough for it not to be in too thick a layer. Put into the oven for 20–25 minutes, stirring two or three times during that period. The less you stir, the more clumps of crumble form, which we like.

Meanwhile, start preparing the plums. Wash and halve them, removing and discarding the pits. Put the plums and granulated sugar into a large wide pan over medium-low heat for 20–30 minutes, stirring every 7 minutes or so, until the plums still hold their shape but are covered in a dark viscous syrup. Avoid stirring too vigorously.

If necessary add sugar to taste—*the riper the plums, the less sugar needed.*

Serve the plums and crumble hot, and separately, so that people can choose the amount of crumble they want on their plums.

Leftover loose crumble stores well and can be used for other purposes—for instance, it pairs well with yogurt or cut fruit.

We speak a lot over the phone but I can't stress the importance of meeting regularly in person. OK, words can be beautiful but sometimes you just need more to get the picture. Body language, glances, screws, and smiles all bring the dramas that develop into a dish. A simple nod of approval can inspire me with confidence, while a murmur of discontent can foster a desire to perfect any work in progress.

I'm mentioning this here because oatcakes are my convenience food at our meetings. I often have a mini pack or two stashed in my bag and always divide them into three. Duval's always grateful. Jacob says he's grown to like them. Whether forced or not, we ate so many together that our local discount store in Deptford sold out of stock! So, as a sort of solution for the hard times, we came up with our own recipe. I added garri, dried and toasted cassava granules, which gives the oatcakes extra crunch.

GARRI OATCAKES

Makes 10 large oatcakes

Time: 1 hour

2½ cups rolled oats

1 teaspoon flaky sea salt

½ cup plus 2 tablespoons garri

¼ cup olive oil

generous ¾ cup very hot water

Preheat the oven to 350°F.

Blend (or grind) the oats until they're powdered. Add the salt and garri and mix. Add the oil and hot water.

Mix until well combined, knead lightly on a clean surface, mound into a ball, and then flatten with a large surface, like the underside of a plate.

Roll the dough further to the desired thickness (⅓ inch) then, using an upturned cup (around 2-inch diameter), cut out as many oatcakes shapes as possible.

Lift each oatcake off the surface with a thin metal spatula, or equivalent.

Shape the excess dough into a ball and repeat the process until the vast majority is oatcake-shaped.

Bake on the middle rack of the oven for 40 minutes, turning once halfway through the cooking time.

Cool completely, then store in an airtight container.

Tamarind is a refreshing and distinctive drink. The fruit itself is a treat, hidden in a firm yet brittle brown pod. It has noticeable fibers and small pips that are eventually discarded after securing the chewy, sweet, and slightly tart, sticky flesh. To reproduce this drink quickly and easily, we use tamarind in its concentrated form. I remember first drinking this juice in Zanzibar, not knowing which of the island's interesting spices and fruits the drink was made from but loving it nonetheless.

TAMARIND WATER

Makes about 6 cups

Time: 7 minutes

6 cups water

2 tablespoons tamarind concentrate

½ cup turbinado sugar

In a saucepan, heat the water. Add the tamarind concentrate and sugar. Once the mixture starts to boil, reduce to low to medium heat and simmer for 5 minutes, until the drink is well combined. Then remove from the heat and pour into a bottle.

Refrigerate and serve cold. This keeps for up to 3 days. Shake well before serving.

menu

YORUBA BANANA | PRICE | #2.00 KG

"From morning to early evening the kitchen was constantly full of people peeling, chopping, and chatting."

When we visited Yemi's family in Lagos there were always a few large containers full of jollof rice and red sauce in our host Auntie Harrisat's fridge. We were encouraged to delve into it throughout the day, and we certainly did. Duval even took to having a breakfast of jollof. From morning to early evening the kitchen was constantly full of people peeling, chopping, and chatting.

The dish is common to many West African countries, and most people familiar with jollof rice will claim to have a "true" recipe, tale, and affection for this incandescent orange rice. We had always intended on developing our own Groundnut version of jollof rice to anchor a menu. Yet jollof is such a contested dish and maybe nothing demonstrates this more than the disputes among ourselves. I came to jollof as an adult via a tiny Yoruba takeout place in New Cross, the closest equivalent I had growing up was pilau rice.

Yemi and Duval have differing versions of what jollof should really be like.

Duval's grandma from Sierra Leone made a rich sauce with ham, sliced red pepper, and onions that runs through the rice. Yemi's Nigerian version involves onions, peppers, and tomatoes blended and cooked down, then used to steam the rice. In Lagos markets we noticed traders using heavy metal motor-driven blenders to produce a vibrant reddy-orange liquid. It's a small-scale operation where people take onions, peppers, and tomatoes to the market and have the ingredients ground to a sauce. Our version sits in between, using techniques from each method to produce what for us is the foolproof version and some of the tastiest jollof rice around.

For this menu, we have paired our jollof rice with some fairly traditional Nigerian dishes—yellow-black fried plantain, or dodo, and moin-moin, a steamed bean dish.

None of us are particularly fond of fizzy drinks, but there are two exceptions. Ginger beer is one. The other is bitter lemon. It appears to have missed out on the evolution of carbonated drink to cans and remains largely in bottle form. Reportedly, it was once very popular in the UK. But in such places as Lagos, Juba, and Freetown you'll still see the iconic bitter lemon nested alongside the more common sodas in bars and shops. And most places you find jollof rice in London, you'll see bitter lemon bottles in the drinks cabinet.

We set out to recreate our own bitter lemon cordial, and while this doesn't have some of the ingredients in the original, such as quinine, this is a delicious and homemade stand-in that satisfies our cravings.

BITTER LEMON CORDIAL

Makes 2 quarts

Time: 1 hour 15 minutes (plus 48 hours steeping)

zest of 3 lemons, 3 oranges and 3 limes

2 cardamom pods

1 sprig of lavender or 1 teaspoon dried lavender leaves

5 cups granulated sugar

4¼ cups squeezed lemon juice (about 25 lemons)

1 cup squeezed orange juice (about 2 oranges)

1 cup squeezed lime juice (about 6 limes)

Add the zest of 1 lemon, 1 orange, and 1 lime; the cardamom pods; and the lavender to 2 cups of water and cover. Allow to steep for 48 hours.

Add the zest of the other 2 lemons, 2 oranges, and 2 limes to 4 cups of warm water in a large pan. Add the sugar and bring to a boil, stirring periodically to help the sugar melt. Once boiling, turn down the heat and simmer for approximately 30 minutes, until a syrup forms. The syrup should coat the back of a spoon but slide off slowly.

Add the lemon, orange, and lime juice to the syrup. Bring to a boil, then reduce to a slow simmer for another 10 minutes. Leave to cool.

Once the steeped liquid has stood for 48 hours, add it to the sugar cordial and mix well. Store in the fridge for up to a month, or freeze.

Serve with 4 parts chilled sparkling water over ice.

SWEET CASHEWS

Serves 4

Time: 20 minutes

2 tablespoons honey

3 tablespoons water

10 ounces cashews

1 tablespoon sea salt flakes

Preheat the oven to 350°F and line a rimmed baking sheet with parchment paper or foil.

Combine the honey and water in a large bowl. Pour in the cashews and stir until they are evenly coated.

Spread the nuts on the baking sheet, evenly spaced apart, and put into the oven for 15–20 minutes, shaking the pan occasionally. The cashews will turn a golden brown color when ready.

Remove from the oven and sprinkle over the salt while hot, shaking the pan vigorously. Serve as a sticky, salty treat.

We once worked in a restaurant where artichoke leaves were summarily discarded. But the leaves act so well as spoons and contain a little tidbit of juicy, earthy-flavored flesh. Perfect to ladle a mouthful of beet anise soup. Ideally use a fresh big-leaved artichoke with no discoloration at the tips.

BEET ANISE SOUP & ARTICHOKE SCOOP

Serves: 4

Time: 45 minutes

6 tablespoons olive oil

4 celery stalks, finely sliced

2 large carrots, coarsely grated

4 cups vegetable stock (see page 313)

2 star anise

3 tablespoons fresh tarragon leaves

1⅓ pounds cooked beets, cut into chunks (juice reserved)

1 teaspoon salt

For the artichoke scoops

2 artichokes

2 bay leaves

Heat the olive oil in a large heavy-bottomed nonstick pan. Add the celery and fry over medium to high heat for 3 minutes. Add the carrots and continue to fry, stirring regularly, for 10 minutes.

Transfer to a deep-sided pan and add the stock, star anise, tarragon, beets (with their juices), and salt. Place over low heat and simmer, covered, for 15 minutes.

Remove 1 star anise, but leave the other one in the pan. Blend the soup, then pass through a fine-mesh sieve. This removes any small pieces of anise bark. Serve warm.

Fill a pan with water big enough to fit both artichokes in comfortably. Add the bay leaves and bring to a boil. If there are sharp thorns or the ends of the artichoke are discolored, snip off with scissors, and cut off the majority of the stem. Once the water boils, reduce to a rolling boil and place in the artichokes.

Depending on their size, cook the artichokes for 25–40 minutes. The leaves loosen as they cook. To check if it is done you can pull at the leaves with tongs to see if they easily come free from the main body of the artichoke. Larger artichokes will take longer. Remove the artichoke and place in a colander. Run briefly under cold water and transfer to a cutting board. With a sharp knife, halve the artichoke and remove the feathery choke in the center. Serve the halved artichoke face down. Peel the artichoke leaf by leaf using it to scoop soup. Once all the leaves have been removed, you can eat the heart.

PICKLED PEPPERS

Makes a 1-quart jar

Time: 40 minutes

4 red bell peppers

1 lemon, quartered

1 halved bulb of garlic

2 tablespoons date molasses

2 Scotch bonnet peppers, halved
and seeded

10 sprigs of fresh thyme

scant 1 cup white wine vinegar

2½ cups water

2 tablespoons salt

scant ¼ cup extra virgin olive oil

Seed the bell peppers and discard the core, then roughly cut them into slices about ¾ inch wide. Put them into a deep pan with all the other ingredients and bring to a boil.

Meanwhile, sterilize a 1-quart glass canning jar.

Once the liquid is boiling, remove the pan from the heat. Take out the solid ingredients from the pan using a slotted spoon, and put them into the sterilized jar. Pour over the liquid.

Seal the jar and store in a cool dry place for at least a week before eating the peppers. They should be spicy and full of flavor.

*In my memory moin-moin is a celebratory dish, something for a special occasion.
It was a fixture at Nigerian parties when we were young, where
our parents danced, danced, and forgot themselves.*

*Traditionally the black-eyed peas are soaked, skinned, and then steamed in banana leaves or in empty
tins that cooks have on hand. I love to see this type of improvisation. It's a way of life to create solutions
instead of buying them. Our moin-moin skips the skinning, which, for us, improves the form and
texture. It has been well received by all who have tried and tasted it, and is an especially good option
for vegetarians hoping to find something new. I hope you get round to making this one.*

MOIN-MOIN

Serves 6–8

**Time: 3 hours 10 minutes
(plus 12 hours soaking)**

9 ounces dried black-eyed peas

2 large red bell peppers

2 cloves of garlic

sunflower oil

1 medium red onion, peeled
and chopped

1 tablespoon tomato paste

1 teaspoon ground ginger

½ teaspoon ground black pepper

¼ teaspoon smoked paprika

½ teaspoon cayenne pepper

1½ teaspoons salt

Soak the black-eyed peas in a large bowl of cold water, covered with plastic wrap, for 12 hours. Drain in a sieve and discard any excess water, then pulse the peas roughly in a food processor.

Preheat the oven to 350°F.

Halve the red peppers and remove the stem and seeds. *It makes sense to roast a few peppers at a time if you have more on hand.* Put the halved peppers on a baking sheet, add the whole garlic cloves, drizzle with a little oil, and roast for 20–30 minutes, or until the skin of the peppers has blackened a little.

Tip the peppers and garlic into a bowl, cover with plastic wrap, and leave to cool for 10 minutes. Leave the oven on. Once cooled, peel the peppers and squeeze the garlic out of the papery shells.

Put all the ingredients into a bowl, add 1 tablespoon of warm water, and mix by hand. Then pulse with a hand blender. Add 1 tablespoon oil and blend again. It should be a smooth silky paste.

Grease a 1-pound loaf pan with a little sunflower oil and add the moin-moin mix. Lightly oil a strip of aluminium foil large enough to cover the pan, and wrap it tightly over to form a lid. The shiny side should face down, since this reflects and retains the heat. Wrap again, both sides and lengthwise, to ensure no heat escapes while the moin-moin is steaming.

Place the loaf pan in a deep roasting pan and pour in warm water until it reaches halfway up the sides of the pan. Steam on the middle rack of the oven for 1 hour and 20 minutes.

Remove from the oven, but leave the pan in the roasting pan of water for another 30 minutes. Then take it out of the water bath and let it rest for another 10 minutes.

Use a bread knife to separate the moin-moin from the sides of the pan. Invert, then shake gently to release completely. It should slide quite easily from the loaf pan. Slice into ¾-inch-thick portions to serve.

*This recipe highlights the colorful stalks of chard and uses beet stalks,
which have a similar flavor to the chard yet are often discarded. The stalks can
be very fibrous, so slicing them finely makes them easy to eat, and tossing them with
a sprinkle of brown sugar and a squeeze of lime sweetens them while encouraging
the beautiful colors of the stalks to bleed through the salad.*

RAINBOW CHARD & BEET STALKS

Serves 4

Time: 11 minutes

a pinch of salt

10 ounces rainbow chard

5 ounces beet stalks

1 teaspoon brown sugar

2 teaspoons lime juice

Bring a medium pan of lightly salted water to the boil.

Meanwhile, trim the leaves off the stalks of the chard and beet and discard the leaves. Wash the stalks with cold water and cut them crosswise into 3- to 5-inch-long pieces.

Boil the stalks for 3 minutes, then drain and rinse under cold water.

Slice the stalks lengthwise into strips as thinly as possible, as this makes the salad more elegant.

Pile the stalks into a serving dish and sprinkle with the brown sugar and lime juice. Toss and serve.

 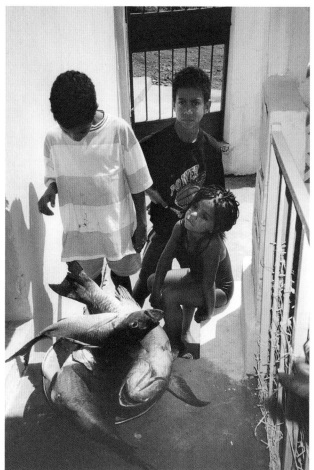

AUNTIE ANNETTE; DUVAL, MILES, AND ISSY WITH LOCAL FISH, FREETOWN, SIERRA LEONE

I loved fish as a child, until my brother Miles declared that it was horrible because it was fishy! Sadly my sister Isabella and I came to agree with him, and we refused to eat anything that had fish in it for years. In those days, my grandma would give us shito and we could not understand why these old peanut butter jars filled with intensely fish-based dark sauce would make our parents so happy.

I have to thank Folayemi's Auntie Annette for bringing shito back into my life as an adult. Now I understand. This rich oily mixture is full of deep flavors that combine to create an enigmatic sauce that can elevate almost any meal. When times are hard I mix it with plain rice or bread and feel like a king.

SHITO

Makes about 2 cups
Time: 1 hour 35 minutes

2 onions, finely diced

extra virgin olive oil

2 tablespoons red palm oil

1 teaspoon salt

1 teaspoon coarsely ground
black pepper

1 heaping teaspoon
ground white pepper

1 teaspoon ground ginger

2 bay leaves

1 teaspoon finely
chopped dried chile

½ teaspoon cayenne pepper

1 Scotch bonnet pepper, finely diced

¾ ounce dried smoked shrimp

2 smoked herring
(or smoked mackerel) fillets

2 cloves of garlic

2 ounces fresh ginger

3 tablespoons tomato paste

1 fresh tomato, finely diced

Fry the onions over medium heat with 2 tablespoons of olive oil for 30 minutes. The onions should caramelize to a dark brown color and soften but not burn. Add the palm oil, salt, black pepper, white pepper, ground ginger, bay leaves, dried chile, cayenne pepper, and Scotch bonnet pepper and continue to fry gently.

Blend or crush the smoked shrimp in a blender until they form a fine powder. Remove the skin and any remaining fine bones from the smoked fillets with tweezers and chop the flesh into ⅓-inch-wide strips. Put to one side.

Peel and chop the garlic and fresh ginger, then crush to a paste. Add the crushed garlic and ginger and the tomato paste to the pot of onions. After 5 minutes, stir in the diced tomato, smoked prawns, and smoked herring.

Turn the heat down to low, cover the pan with a lid, and cook for 40 minutes, stirring every 5 minutes. Take off the heat when the sauce is thick and dark brown in color.

Remove the bay leaves, then decant the sauce into a clean sealable jar and top up with a layer of olive oil (3 to 4 tablespoons). *Ensuring that there is a surface layer of oil helps to preserve the sauce for as long as possible, therefore tall narrow jars are best for storage.*

Serve at room temperature. The shito will keep for 2 weeks in a refrigerator or cool place away from direct sunlight. If the top of the sauce looks dry, add more extra virgin olive oil.

For me there are few more exciting dishes to be served than a whole grilled fish. It is particularly special if served in sight of a river or coast, where it is always best, since freshness is key. Snapper is a good fish to cook whole, and with some cooked-down sweet onions and peppers and a touch of hot pepper, you have a killer combo.

RED SNAPPER

Serves 4

Time: 30 minutes

1 medium red snapper, scaled and cleaned

2¼ teaspoons sea salt, plus extra for seasoning

1 Scotch bonnet pepper

1 teaspoon freshly ground black pepper

2 tablespoons olive oil

2 onions

1 green bell pepper

2 tablespoons peanut oil

2 cloves of garlic, finely sliced

a pinch of granulated sugar

fresh lemon wedges, to serve

Cut three slits at an angle across the body of the snapper on each side. Sprinkle with 2 teaspoons of sea salt and massage it well into the fish, making sure you push it into any crevices. Put the fish into a dish or pan.

Remove the seeds from the Scotch bonnet pepper and cut it into quarters. Put three of the pepper quarters into the cavity of the fish, and set the remaining quarter aside for later. Sprinkle the black pepper over the fish and pour over the olive oil. Leave the fish to rest for 45 minutes (if putting into the fridge, return it to room temperature 15 minutes before cooking).

Preheat the broiler. Slice the onions, green pepper, and the remaining quarter of the Scotch bonnet pepper. Heat the peanut oil in a frying pan and add the garlic. Cook for a couple of minutes, then add the Scotch bonnet pepper followed by the onions and green pepper. Cook for 10 minutes over low to medium heat, until the onions just start to turn translucent and the peppers begin to soften.

In the meantime begin cooking the fish. Remove it from the dish or pan it was resting in, reserving any juices, and place it under the broiler for 7 minutes.

After the onions have been cooking for 10 minutes, add the sugar and ¼ teaspoon of salt. Cook over low heat for another 5 minutes, then turn off the heat and cover.

Turn the fish over and cook on the other side for another 7 minutes. Turn the fish once more, then, using a pastry brush, coat the fish with some of the juices reserved from marinating the fish. Cook for another 2–3 minutes, then flip the fish and do the same with the other side.

Put the onions and peppers on a serving dish. Remove the Scotch bonnet peppers from the cavity and place the fish on top of the vegetables. Season with sea salt and black pepper and serve with rice and lemon wedges.

As yellow plantain ripens, its skin turns black. In this state, it could be mistaken for being overripe or rotten. However, at this stage it is, in many ways, at its best. Natural sugars develop that, when fried, caramelize into golden treats like no other. In Nigeria, dodo is a classic cut from the same compilation as moin-moin. Cubed and spiced yellow-black plantains are known as kelewele in Ghana. They can also be sliced into elegant discs, which is how we prefer them.

FRIED PLANTAIN/DODO

Serves 4

Time: 25 minutes

2 yellow-black plantains

1 level teaspoon cayenne pepper

a pinch of salt

about 1¼ cups sunflower oil, for frying

Top and tail the plantains, then make a skin-deep incision all the way along the spine of each one. Open the skin and remove the flesh. Slice diagonally into long discs roughly ⅓ inch thick and 3 inches long.

Put the plantain into a large bowl and add the cayenne pepper and a pinch of salt. Gently massage with your hands so that each piece is equally covered with seasoning. Be gentle, because the plantain can turn to mush if too much pressure is applied.

Pour the sunflower oil into a wide frying pan until it's about ⅛ inch deep (note that when you put the plantain in, the oil level will rise further). Put the frying pan over medium heat. While the oil heats up, prepare a surface, rack, or plate covered with paper towels.

When the oil is hot, test it with one of the plantain discs—it should sizzle. Fry the plantain in batches by placing the discs in the frying pan face down, one by one. The oil should sizzle and you will see small bubbles around each disc. If this does not happen, leave more time for the oil to heat up or increase the heat—frying on a very low heat will create oily plantain. Do not let the discs overlap in the pan. It's likely that you will need to fry them in batches, depending on the size of the pan you use.

After 3–4 minutes, turn over each disc using tongs or a spatula. The plantain should be golden brown on the outside. The thinnest parts, around the edge of each disc, will fry much more quickly, and will therefore crisp up and turn darker. However, the plantain should not char. Fry on the second side for 3–4 minutes.

Remove the discs from the pan one by one when each piece is cooked, and leave to rest on paper towels. Serve hot.

Leave the oil to cool, then store in a sealed container. It can be used again to fry plantain and will keep for a long time.

Selecting plantains is an important part of the process prior to preparation. If you want a sweeter plantain, look for ones that have a strong contrast between the yellow base-color and the black streaks on the skin. Also make sure you feel the plantain. It should have a decent weight, and not be mushy under the skin when you squeeze it gently. It's easier to select a yellow plantain, although the same principles apply. Some people prefer yellow plantains, which have more body and aren't as sweet. I'm a big fan of the yellow-black ones, though. I can't get enough of them.

BAKED PLANTAIN

Serves 4

Time: 25 minutes

4 yellow or yellow-black plantains

To prepare, top and tail your plantains, make a skin-deep incision, and peel. Open up your plantains, halve lengthwise, and bake at 395°F for 15 minutes or so on a lightly oiled baking sheet with the curved side facing down. Yellow plantains will need a little longer to cook through.

This is the dish that first got me into cooking. Talking about it got me my first job in a kitchen, and together with the help of friends, local restaurants, and family it's the recipe we have worked on the most for this book, because we all know how good it should be.

If I could only eat one thing in the world it would probably be my grandma's jollof. She would regularly cook a big pot with care and patience and insist that everyone took home a small container of it. Cooking the rice and storing it for the following day or to give to friends to take away is part of a sharing culture that surrounds jollof—just remember to return the Tupperware!

JOLLOF RICE

Serves 4

Time: 1 hour 20 minutes

4 red bell peppers

2 medium to large onions

3 bulbs of garlic

2 teaspoons salt

½ a Scotch bonnet pepper

¼ pound plum tomatoes

¼ cup sunflower oil

1 teaspoon dried thyme

½ teaspoon ground ginger

½ teaspoon cayenne pepper
or alternative

¼ teaspoon smoked paprika

1 heaping teaspoon tomato paste

generous 2 cups chicken stock
(see page 314)

1 teaspoon red palm oil

1¼ cups white basmati rice
(to 2½ cups of cooking sauce;
the ratio is 1:2 of rice
to cooking sauce)

Finely slice the peppers and onions. Make a paste out of the garlic and 1 teaspoon of salt. Seed and slice the Scotch bonnet pepper, dice the tomatoes, and set them aside.

Soften the onions and peppers in the sunflower oil over high heat for 5 minutes, stirring frequently. Add the pasted garlic, Scotch bonnet pepper, tomatoes, and dry seasonings and cook for another 10 minutes over medium heat, stirring frequently.

Add the tomato paste, cook for another minute or so, then remove from the heat. Blend the mixture with a generous ¾ cup of chicken stock. *If this was prepared in advance, reheat it first.*

Add another ¾ cup of stock and blend until the mixture is smooth. Add the palm oil, a final teaspoon of salt, and then pour 2½ cups of this mixture back into the pot. Heat the sauce until it is lightly bubbling.

Measure out your rice, then add to the pot. *The pot should have a tight-fitting lid, but if it doesn't you can use some foil with the shiny side facing down to retain the heat.*

Stir gently so that all the rice is coated with the red sauce, then reduce the heat to a very low flame—the lowest possible. Cover and simmer for 10 minutes. Open the lid and stir gently again. *It is important to get under the center of the pan so all the rice cooks at the same rate.* Cover and simmer for another 10 minutes. Open and stir for a final time, then simmer for a final 10 minutes. This makes 30 minutes cooking time in total.

Turn the heat off and allow to steam, covered, for another 15 minutes. *It's tempting to open the pot here but it's very important to trust the process and allow the rice to cook residually.* This improves the final taste and texture of the rice.

Open the lid then leave to stand for 5 minutes, uncovered. Then fluff with a fork to separate the rice, slowly working inward from the edge of the pan in a swirling motion. *If the rice is not completely cooked, add the remaining ½ cup stock, stir gently, then place back over low heat for another 10 minutes.*

Spoon the rice out onto a separate dish and serve.

People make jollof in different ways, incorporating preferred cooking techniques and local ingredients to their personal recipes, similar to how a paella or biryani might adapt to different regions or local traditions. Something that distinguishes the jollof that I am most familiar with is the delicious meat sauce that accompanies it. The sauce ingredients echo those in the rice, and it's banging with chicken.

JOLLOF SAUCE

Serves 4

Time: 1 hour 50 minutes

4 onions

3 red bell peppers

1 small whole chicken
(about 2 pounds)

2 teaspoons salt

1 teaspoon black pepper

1 teaspoon fresh
thyme leaves

scant ¼ cup olive oil

1 Scotch bonnet pepper

2 fresh tomatoes

4 cloves of garlic

2 tablespoons
tomato paste

generous ¾ cup vegetable stock
(see page 313)

Finely slice the onions and bell peppers. Chop the chicken into 12 pieces, skin them, and trim off any fat. Using your hands, mix the chicken with the salt, pepper, and thyme.

Fry the chicken pieces in the oil with a whole Scotch bonnet pepper over medium heat for 15 minutes, turning them every 4 minutes. Ensure each piece has room to move. Once the chicken is nicely browned, remove from the pan and put to one side.

Add the onions and bell peppers to the pan and fry them for 20 minutes, stirring occasionally.

Meanwhile, bring a small pan of water to the boil. Gently slit the skins of the tomatoes and drop them into the boiling water. When the skin begins to come away from the flesh, take them out and peel away the skin with your hands.

Crush the garlic and finely chop the skinned tomatoes. Stir the crushed garlic, chopped tomatoes, and tomato paste into the pan of sauce, then turn the heat to low and cook for 10 minutes.

Return the chicken to the pan, pour in the stock, and cook for another 15 minutes. Taste and season with salt if necessary. Serve hot.

LADY IN DISGUISE

Makes 24 muffins

Time: 1 hour

3¼ cups all-purpose flour

1 teaspoon baking powder

¾ teaspoon baking soda

¼ teaspoon ground mace

¼ teaspoon ground ginger

½ teaspoon fine sea salt

7 ounces okra

2 Rocha (or Comice) pears

⅔ cup dandelion and burdock soft drink

⅓ cup fresh pear juice or apple cider

4 ounces unsalted butter, plus extra for greasing

¾ cup superfine sugar

2 medium free-range eggs

For the glaze

⅓ cup unsalted butter

scant ½ cup dandelion and burdock soft drink

3 tablespoons elderflower cordial

5 tablespoons powdered sugar

2 tablespoons pear and okra mixture (from preparation of muffins, see above)

8 fresh strawberries, sliced

Preheat the oven to 350°F. Grease a 24-cup mini-muffin tin well to ensure that the muffins won't stick.

Sift the flour, baking powder, baking soda, mace, ginger, and salt into a large mixing bowl. Set aside.

Prepare the okra by removing the very top of each one, which is a little fibrous. Then peel and core the pears. In a food processor, blend the okra with the pears, dandelion and burdock drink, and pear or apple juice. *Don't be alarmed; it should have a fresh-flavored gooey texture.* Set 2 tablespoons of the mixture aside to use in the glaze.

Melt the butter in a pan over gentle heat and pour into a bowl. Stir in the sugar. Add the eggs one at a time and whisk until well combined.

Add the flour mix to the butter, sugar, and egg. Then rub together until you see no flour remaining. *It is important not to overmix here. If you do so, there's a risk that the muffins won't rise properly.*

Finally add the okra and pear blend, again mixing briefly. *There should be marblelike swirls of green and white.* Leave to rest for 5 minutes.

Spoon the batter into the cups of the mini-muffin tin until it is level with the rim of each cup. Bake for 25 minutes.

While the muffins are baking you can prepare the glaze. Put the butter and the dandelion and burdock drink into a nonstick pan over a very high heat. Bring to a boil, then boil for 2 minutes. It should reduce slightly.

Turn the heat down to medium and add the elderflower cordial. Next sift in the powdered sugar, stirring as you go along. Finally, add the reserved 2 tablespoons of pear and okra blend and stir until completely dissolved. Cook over low heat for 5 minutes.

Remove from the heat and set aside to rest. The glaze will continue to thicken slightly off the heat. After 25 minutes, insert a toothpick into a muffin to test if they are done; it will come out clean when the muffins are ready. Remove them from the oven and take them out of their tin as soon as possible, otherwise they may stick. Cool on a wire rack.

Once the glaze and muffins are completely cool, glaze the muffins. Garnish with a slice of fresh strawberry and serve.

This is a cool and refreshing dessert option. You can make it with a savory stock to create a simple starter too.

CASHEW MILK

Serves 6

Time: 40 minutes (plus 12 hours soaking)

1 pound raw unsalted cashews

3 quarts water

½ teaspoon fine sea salt

1 tablespoon sugar

1 whole nutmeg

Soak the cashews in the water for 12 hours or overnight.

Drain and rinse the cashews, then add 2 cups of fresh cold water.

Transfer the cashews to a blender and blend thoroughly for 3 minutes, resting for a minute after each minute of blending. It's important to do this because your blender is likely to burn out if you overwork it.

Take a 5-minute break to rest the blender, then add another 2 cups of water and repeat the blending process.

Add a final 2 cups of water, the salt and sugar, and then blend for a final time. The texture should be smooth, between the consistency of milk and cream.

Ladle into a bowl and grate whole nutmeg over the soup.

Serve chilled.

It would have been a shame if this book hadn't featured chocolate at all. West Africa accounts for a large proportion of global cocoa bean production, with whole islands like São Tomé once dedicated to its cultivation. That said, apart from legendary chocolate malt drinks like Milo and Bournville, as far as my experience goes there's no firm culture of chocolate consumption in the places I've visited across West Africa.

DARK CHOCOLATE BAR

Makes one 3½-ounce bar

Time: 2 hours

3½ ounces cacao nibs

2 tablespoons turbinado brown sugar

pinch sea salt

½ ounce cacao butter

You'll need a single blade electric coffee grinder and a solid pestle and mortar to make this.

Preheat the oven to 275°F. Put the cacao nibs on a baking sheet and roast for 10 minutes. As you remove the nibs, place a pestle and mortar in the oven.

Using a single blade electric coffee grinder, blend the sugar and salt to a very fine powder. Add the roasted nibs and blend all together until it becomes a fluid mass. It will need around 5 minutes of action—be sure to rest the grinder after every minute or so to stop it overheating.

Melt the cacao butter in a double boiler and add to the blended nibs. Remove the pestle and mortar from the oven and help the mixture into it. "Grind" the chocolaty fluid for at least 10 minutes. This process is called "conching" and helps meld the flavors.

Pour the mixture into a chocolate mold, or a 1-pound loaf pan. Leave for 30 minutes at room temperature, then place in the fridge for another 30 minutes so that it can set completely.

menu

"Inspired, we felt there was the perfect opportunity to serve food the way we knew it should be."

Jacob and I were skeptical. We had good times at St. John's Hall, and perhaps a change of scenery was in order. But to go from a small kitchen to no kitchen seemed a major step. Plugging the gap, Duval sketched these ingenious collapsible surfaces that could be transported freely from one place to another. He came to the studio armed with a little model demonstrating how it would work, and we were sold on the idea. The notion of a pop-up was reaching new levels. We were moving to Lewisham Arthouse.

The Arthouse gallery is a space with clean and clear potential. They had never handled food in the building, so there was excitement and anticipation from both sides about how we could make it work. November 2012 to July 2013 was our lengthiest period without doing an event, so we set two weeks—our longest run—for the dinners. We knew the time frame would be a challenge, but one with important outcomes. The larger space meant that we were now able to share our food with a new crowd, without rejecting the pillars that had supported us throughout the previous year.

As Duval brought his model kitchen to life, building, stretching and drilling, Jacob and I slipped off for some culinary research. Given the situation, a menu that could be assembled easily on site was in order.

During the experimental phase, I opened tab after tab on my Internet search engine, scouring online sources for different grains and flours. We knew a type of flatbread would be ideal for this menu, and Jacob suggested injera, the national staple of Ethiopia and Eritrea. I was really keen to try it for myself, so set a date to check out a restaurant.

It was great. Slightly vinegary and tart but combined well with mellow, rich flavors. Our trip also reaffirmed the emphasis on handling your food, a tactility that we're all familiar with as it's common to dining all over Africa. We'd discussed guests eating with their hands before, but it took us some time to find the confidence to share the idea. We were conscious that no cutlery might be a step too far, providing an overwhelmingly new experience, but, inspired, we felt there was the perfect opportunity to serve food the way we knew it should be.

When it came to the food, we wanted to take our favorite elements of Ethiopian food but add an extra dimension. The bed of injera and the classic dish wot were absolute musts, though.

Doro wot is served with a piece of chicken and boiled egg, but we made a vegetarian version from slow-cooked onions and niter kibbeh. The fresh turmeric red lentils with roasted sweet potatoes had enough body to contrast with the injera. And the crunchy salad and blanched and peeled cherry tomatoes tossed in fresh dill added a fresh and cooling touch.

The starter was a trio of "small chops" with myriad temperatures, tastes and textures. A common thread was the fruitiness, from the kiwi ice pop to the yellow tomato, orange, and ginger soup. It was mid-July and the middle of the heat wave and we really wanted to lighten the mood of the meal.

Always eager to document the occasion, Duval came across Sophie Davidson's photographs and invited her to shoot one of our dinners. As soon as those films were developed—wow. Everything changed. Since then Sophie has become an integral part of the family, quietly capturing beautiful images at our events and beyond.

*I always wondered why a country as large as Nigeria has no
national spirit. It's famous for its export-strength Guinness and the
local palm wine made from the fermented sap of the palm tree to get
merry and jubilate.*

*Alcohol has a long history as an offering on social occasions. It oils conversation,
building relations, both old and new, and I'm sure it's responsible for many friends
becoming family. Yet the high-percentage drink—the hot water, owing to the
burning sensation when you drink it neat—has always been imported. It started
with European merchants as early as the fifteenth century, though Sharia law in
the Islamic north of the country prohibited consumption and curtailed its advance.
Consequently it was distributed throughout the east, west, and south, closer to the
coast, and closer to the potential for direct trade.*

*Traditional European gin was the most popular of all the spirits in Nigeria. In
1927 imports outgunned those of other international spirits like today's favorite,
cognac. Trade plummeted between 1927 and 1934, although prices for imported
gin remained fixed while local incomes dipped in line with global depression. By
accident or design, such times always coincide with opportunity and some innovators
brought the distillation method—and perhaps a sense of rebellion—back from their
travels in the U.S. where alcohol had famously been prohibited. They sold on their
expertise to other traders, and momentum brewed from the ground up. Soon "illicit
gin," or ogorogoro, production was rife, particularly in the east of the country.*

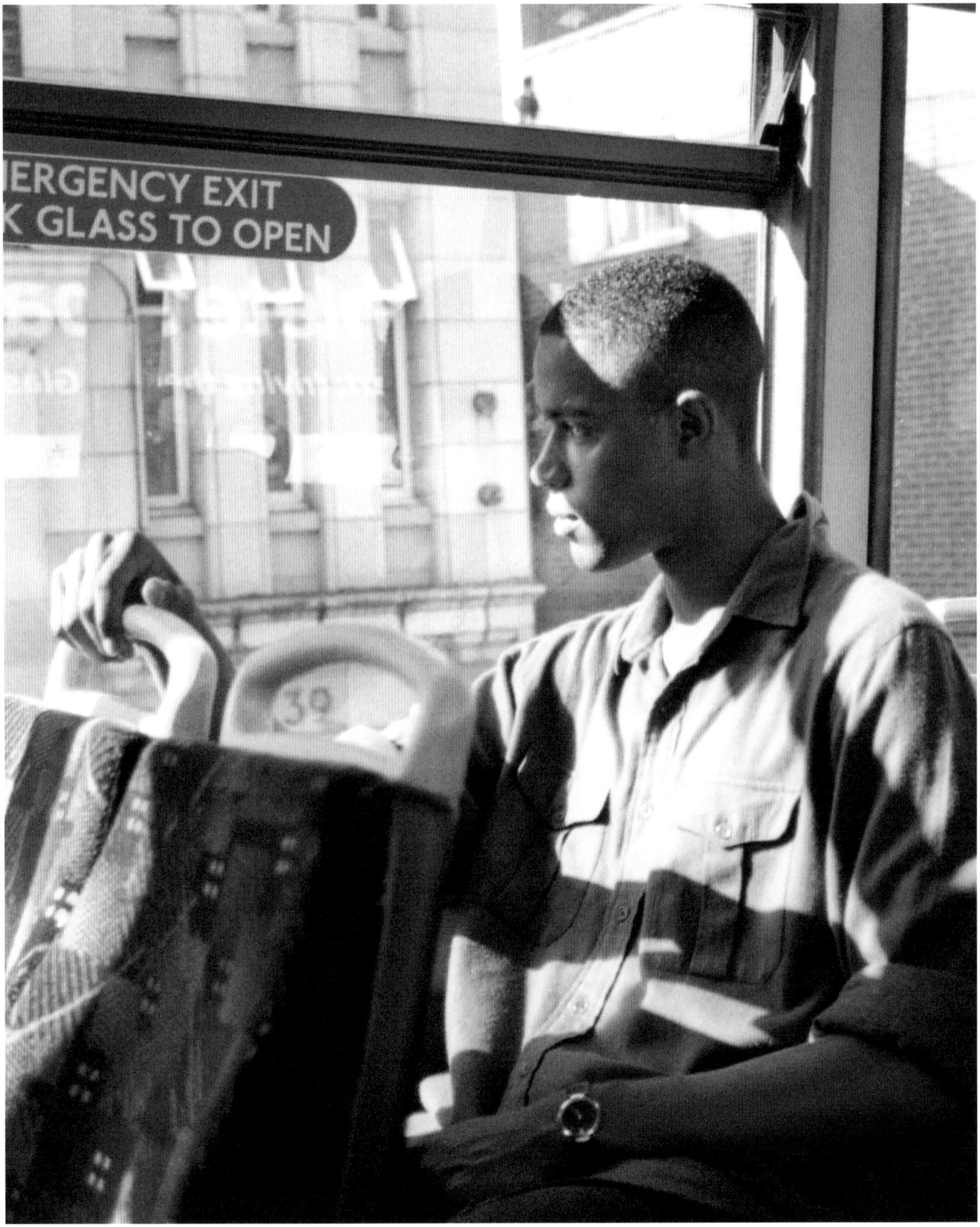
ERGENCY EXIT
K GLASS TO OPEN

In homage to gin days we created this iced tea cocktail.

TEA BITTERS

Makes about 1 quart

Time: 5 minutes (plus 2 hours chilling)

12 breakfast tea bags

generous 1 cup boiling water

generous 1 cup cold water

scant ½ cup dry white vermouth

scant ½ cup gin

generous 1 cup bitter lemon

scant ¼ cup elderflower cordial

fresh lemon wedges, to serve

Add the tea bags to the boiling water. Leave to brew for 10 minutes, then remove. *The tea can be intensely bitter if it stands for too long.*

Add the cold water, then cool completely in the refrigerator or an ice bath to speed up the process. Leave the tea mixture in the fridge for 2 hours, to chill.

To make the tea bitters, mix all the liquid ingredients together and serve over ice, with lemon wedges or lemon ice cubes (see page 319).

Tomatoes are good, but yellow ones always seem a little special.

This soup works best as a shot, which became something of an infatuation after we had one for the first time in Vienna. The orange juice brightens this upbeat blend, and the little matchsticks of ginger give it a pleasant kick.

YELLOW TOMATO SOUP

Serves 10–12

Time: 35 minutes

1 celery stalk

1 large carrot

2 tablespoons olive oil

1¾ pounds yellow plum tomatoes

1 teaspoon ground ginger

1 teaspoon ground white pepper

1 teaspoon sea salt flakes

scant ¼ cup vegetable stock (see page 313)

1 ounce fresh ginger

⅔ cup freshly squeezed orange juice (2 large oranges)

Finely slice the celery and coarsely grate the carrot. Fry in the olive oil over medium heat in a large pan for 10 minutes, or until softened.

Add the yellow tomatoes, ginger, white pepper, sea salt, and stock, and simmer gently for 10 minutes. Blend the soup. Leave to cool, then refrigerate for at least 20 minutes.

Peel the fresh ginger, then quarter lengthwise. Slice into very thin julienned strips, 1 inch long.

Add the orange juice to the soup and stir well. Portion into shot glasses and garnish each one with 2 slices of julienned ginger.

Serve cold.

You'll need some lollipop sticks for this recipe. We found some interesting yellow serving sticks that worked well at dinner, but if worse comes to worst you can use cocktail sticks.

KIWI ICE POP

Makes 8–12 pops

Time: 5 minutes (plus 3 hours freezing time)

4 kiwi fruits

Top and tail the kiwis. To peel them, gently push a teaspoon under the skin of the kiwi and follow the inside of the skin until it reaches about halfway down the fruit. Revolve the spoon in a circular motion around the flesh of the kiwi so that the flesh is separated from the skin.

Remove the teaspoon, turn the kiwi the other way up and apply the same technique until the flesh is entirely separate from the skin. Carefully push the base of the flesh of the kiwi out of the skin. It should slip out fairly easily. If necessary nick the skin with a knife.

Slice the kiwi crosswise into two or three thick slices. *The intricate pattern of the middle of the kiwi should be on show on the cross section.* Slowly insert a lollipop stick into the edge of the kiwi until it reaches the middle.

Put the kiwi slices into a container and place in the freezer, with a little bit of space around them so that they don't stick together. Freeze for at least 3 hours.

Before serving, remove from the freezer and allow to rest at room temperature for 5 minutes.

MUSTARD SHRIMP

Serves 4
Time: 5 minutes

2 cloves of garlic

2 tablespoons olive oil

1 pound peeled raw jumbo shrimp

1 teaspoon chili flakes

1 teaspoon sea salt

juice of 1 lemon

1 tablespoon yellow
mustard seeds

¾ cup chopped fresh parsley

Finely slice the garlic and fry in the oil for 1 minute over medium-low heat. Turn the temperature up to high and add the shrimp, chili flakes, and salt.

Cook for 2 minutes, then add the lemon juice and mustard seeds. Cook for a final minute, then toss with the parsley and serve.

This simple salad is light, fresh, and tactile. It goes very well with fish.
Kohlrabi can be visually intimidating but it is an easy ingredient to use.
If you can't get hold of it, you can use broccoli stalks or turnips as a
substitute. It's important to search for a very hard, green,
unripe mango to achieve a crunchy salad.

MANGO KOHLRABI SALAD

Serves 4
Time: 10 minutes

1 kohlrabi (14 ounces)
1 green mango (14 ounces)

Trim the stalks of the kohlrabi and peel off the skin. Make sure to remove enough skin so that you are left with just the flesh of the vegetable. The area just underneath the skin is quite tough.

Cut the kohlrabi into thin slices roughly ⅛ inch wide. Take a few slices at a time, turn them on their side, and cut them into long strips. Put to one side.

Peel the mango. Cut off the sides of the mango and remove as much flesh from the pit as possible. Cut the flesh into long thin slices the same width as the kohlrabi. Turn a few slices on their side at a time and cut into long strips.

Toss the mango and kohlrabi together and serve.

After many weeks of exploration with plenty of different flours and many failed batches, we finally settled on an injera pikelet, a recipe whose technique and preparation borrows partly from injera and partly from enlarged crumpets—pikelets. It was an achievable compromise that didn't take seven days to ferment—or call for capturing wild yeast— like some recipes we had come across.

INJERA PIKELET

Serves 6

Time: 35 minutes (plus 2 hours 30 minutes resting time)

2 teaspoons granulated sugar

1⅔ cups light soy milk (it's important you get the light version—with regular soy milk the batter doesn't behave in the same way)

2 tablespoons active dry yeast

2½ cups bread flour

1¼ cups fine rice flour

2 teaspoons salt

1 teaspoon baking soda

Mix the sugar, soy milk, and a generous ¾ cup of boiling water in a bowl and stir in the yeast. Cover, then leave in a warm place for 15 minutes.

Combine the flours with the salt. Stir in the yeast liquid and mix until smooth. Cover and leave in a warm place for at least 2 hours.

Mix the baking soda with 1¼ cups of warm water and stir it into the batter. Cover and leave in a warm place for 30 minutes. *The mixture should be the consistency of a thin pancake batter, and bubbles should be starting to form on the surface.* If it is too thick, add a little more warm water and whisk to combine.

Cover a clean clear work surface with paper towels, for the injera to rest on after cooking. Preheat a 13-inch nonstick pan over medium heat, then add a ladleful of the batter. Swirl the pan quickly to evenly coat the bottom, much as you would if making a pancake. Cook on one side for about 2 minutes. You only need to cook one side of the injera. As the pikelet cooks, gently slide a spatula under the side, working your way around the perimeter. This helps to stop it sticking. *Little pockets of air should form on the surface as it cooks.* Gently lift the pikelet off the pan and continue with the rest of the batter, wiping the pan with a dry cloth after every few pikelets to keep the surface clean.

When they are completely cool, you can stack any leftovers and wrap them in plastic wrap. They'll keep for a day at room temperature.

The great thing about this recipe is that it is made almost exclusively with onions. They're cooked down over a few hours, with the simple addition of some spices and niter kibbeh, a spiced clarified butter used widely in Ethiopian cuisine. Wot translates roughly from Amharic as "sauce," we're told, so has a fairly wide interpretation. This version goes perfectly with our injera pikelet, or with actual injera, if you can get your hands on some.

Wot is best when the flavors are left to settle, so ideally make this the day before eating, although it can also be served straightaway.

WOT

Serves 4

Time: 3 hours 15 minutes

1¾ pounds onions

1 ounce fresh ginger

1 ounce garlic

2 tablespoons olive oil

1½ tablespoons niter kibbeh (spiced clarified butter)

2 tablespoons berbere spice blend

1 teaspoon nigella seeds

1 tablespoon salt

4 hard-boiled eggs

Finely dice the onions. Put them into a large pan over low heat for 45 minutes to 1 hour, stirring every 10–15 minutes. Do not add any oil or butter. The onions should be layered high in order to stop them drying out and sticking, so use a narrow pan if that's easier. If they continue to stick, you might add a touch of water.

Peel, slice, and crush the ginger and garlic and set aside.

Once the onions have completely cooked down (after about 45 minutes), add the ginger and garlic. After a couple more minutes, add the olive oil. Cook for another 5 minutes, then add the niter kibbeh, followed by the berbere spice blend and nigella seeds. Cook for 1 hour, stirring frequently.

After 1 hour add the salt, boiled eggs, and stir, then turn off the heat and leave to stand.

It's important to use fresh turmeric root in this recipe. It has a wonderful aroma, with hints of citrus that are lost in the powdered form. You may want to have ready some disposable gloves and an apron, because it can stain very easily. The taste of this dish improves with standing time and into the next day.

FRESH TURMERIC RED LENTILS

Serves 8

Time: 45 minutes

1 pound medium sweet potatoes

scant 2 tablespoons coconut oil

1 teaspoon fine sea salt

1 teaspoon hot paprika

½ teaspoon smoked paprika

½ teaspoon chili powder

¾ ounce fresh turmeric

generous 2 cups vegetable stock (see page 313)

5 ounces fresh plum tomatoes

3½ ounces red lentils (preferably whole, unsplit, skin-on)

Preheat the oven to 395°F.

Peel the sweet potatoes, halve them lengthwise, and cut crosswise at 1-inch intervals. You should now have rough half-moon discs. Put them into a large bowl.

Melt the coconut oil if it's solid, then smother it over the sweet potatoes. Add the salt and dried spices and rub well with your hands so they are evenly distributed. Put them on a baking sheet, place in the oven in the top third, and set a timer for 15 minutes, turning the sweet potatoes after about 7 minutes.

In the meantime prepare the lentils. Peel the fresh turmeric with a teaspoon. *We find that much like ginger it's easier to get into the crevices and minimize wastage this way.* Pound with a pestle and mortar until it becomes a fine, juicy paste.

Add the stock, tomatoes, and fresh turmeric to a deep pot. Place over medium heat.

Rinse the lentils in a fine-mesh sieve and add to the pan. Gently bring to a boil, then simmer over low heat, covered, for 8 minutes. Do not leave for longer than this without checking, because lentils can overcook quickly.

Check the sweet potatoes. You want them so that you can put a fork through each piece with ease. They should taste spicy, salty, and sweet from the caramelization.

Check your lentils. *They are ready when they are translucent, without sunburnt orange spots of the original color at the core.* The stock will reduce significantly as the lentils absorb water. Remove from the heat.

When the sweet potatoes are done, add them to the lentils and fold them into the mix. Serve warm, and reheat over very low temperature so the lentils don't overcook.

Some things are best when you don't do much to them. Rolled in sea salt flakes and dropped into hot oil, sea bream is incredibly tasty. The light, meaty flesh comes away from the fish's skeleton easily and some of the finer bones become brittle and crunchy enough to eat. The fresher the fish, the better, and the quality of sea salt you use will shine through. The fishmonger should scale and gut the sea bream for you.

SEA BREAM

Serves 4

**Time: 20 minutes
(plus 6 minutes per fish)**

1 lemon

2 whole sea bream, porgies,
or dorade

2 tablespoons sea salt flakes, plus
a pinch for serving

2 quarts sunflower oil, for frying

Halve the lemon and wash the fish, using each half of the lemon like a sponge. Look out for any scales that are still on the fish and pay special attention to washing inside the open cavity of the fish's belly.

With a sharp knife, chop each fish in half into head and tail pieces; remove the head if you wish. Place the pieces in a bowl and sprinkle with the salt. With your hands, massage the salt evenly into the fish, then cover and leave to marinate in a cool place for 15 minutes.

In a deep pan or deep-fryer, bring the sunflower oil to 375°F. *Make sure you use a pan that is deep enough, so that the oil is not in danger of overflowing, and always attend the cooking process.*

Fry one piece of fish at a time by gently placing the fish in the hot oil, using tongs or a slotted spoon to ensure you do not splash any oil onto your hands and arms. Make sure the fish is completely submerged and leave to fry for 6 minutes.

When the fish is golden in color and slightly crispy, remove it from the oil with tongs and place it on a rack lined with paper towels to drain. The fish should darken in color slightly as it rests. Repeat this process for each piece of fish.

Lightly sprinkle with a pinch of sea salt and serve hot.

This is a fun and bright dish with a sweet and juicy taste. The fresh dill emits an incredible aroma as soon as it is chopped. Blanching the tomatoes creates a beautiful salad with an unusual texture and also sweetens them. Although any kind of tomato will work for this recipe, plum or cherry tomatoes with a deep red color are best.

TOMATO & DILL

Serves 4

Time: 14 minutes

1 pound ice,
for chilling the tomatoes

1¼ pounds cherry tomatoes or
plum tomatoes

10 sprigs of fresh dill

1 tablespoon olive oil

sea salt flakes

Prepare a bowl of cold water, add the ice, and put to one side.

In a pan, bring roughly 1 quart of water to a boil.

With a sharp knife, make a light incision across the skin of each tomato, trying not to cut too deeply. This allows the skin to come away from the flesh of the tomato when they are put into hot water.

Place the tomatoes in boiling water for 2 minutes. You should soon begin to notice the skin coming away from the flesh. Drain the tomatoes and place in the bowl of ice water. Gently push the skin of each tomato away from the flesh and place the peeled tomatoes in a bowl.

Rip the dill leaves away from the main stalks and roughly chop at ⅓-inch intervals. Throw the dill over the tomatoes and gently toss. *Because the tomatoes have been boiled, they will be quite soft. Be careful not to crush them.*

Drizzle with the oil, then sprinkle a pinch of sea salt flakes over the salad and serve.

BAKED BROCCOLI FALAFEL

Makes 24
Preparation time: 1 hour

3 cups cooked chickpeas

1 head of broccoli

¼ cup olive oil

2 medium carrots

1 tablespoon cumin seeds

⅔ cup garri

4 cloves of garlic, chopped

1 tablespoon salt

If you are starting with dried chickpeas, soak them for 8 hours. Drain, boil them rapidly in a change of water for 15 minutes, then simmer over low heat for 1 hour.

Preheat the oven to 425°F. Line a baking sheet with parchment paper and oil it lightly.

Holding the broccoli florets in one hand, remove as much stalk as possible in a clean slice. Set the stalk aside. *When cut into long matchsticks, it can be added to the mango and kohlrabi salad.* Chop the broccoli florets quite evenly. *This is just to ease the blending.*

Put the cooked chickpeas and the raw chopped broccoli into a blender with the olive oil and pulse together. Finely grate the carrot. Grind the cumin seeds until relatively fine.

Combine all the ingredients and mix well. Divide the mixture into 24 compact evenly sized balls, then apply a little bit of pressure to the top of each one. They should flatten slightly and take on a nugget shape. Use your fingers to round the edges of each falafel.

Place the falafel on the prepared baking sheet and bake for 30 minutes in the top third of the oven, turning once at the halfway stage. They will brown slightly when they're ready.

Serve the falafel with tomato and dill (see page 218) wrapped in flatbreads.

Making this malleable dough is a very hands-on joyful experience. Our recipe creates a zesty, fragrant, and sweet pastry that is cookie-like when cooked.

Pastry has varied properties at different temperatures; heat from your hands and the environment can quickly warm it up, making it sticky and inconsistent. From the moment you bring your dough out of the fridge to when it goes into the oven, it is important to work quickly. If you bake regularly, it's also worth making lots of dough and freezing some to use in the future. Remember to take it out of the freezer and put it into the fridge for 12 hours before using it.

SWEET PASTRY

Makes enough for two 8-inch edible fruit bowls

Time: 1 hour 20 minutes (plus 4 hours chilling)

1 ounce fresh ginger

½ cup plus 1 tablespoon powdered sugar

scant 2½ cups all-purpose flour, plus a little extra

zest of 5 limes and/or lemons

⅔ cup dark brown sugar

6 tablespoons cold salted butter

2 medium eggs

1 teaspoon lime or lemon juice

Peel the ginger and crush to a paste, using a strong knife or a fine grater.

In a large bowl, mix the powdered sugar, flour, ginger, citrus zest, and dark brown sugar.

Slice the cold butter into very thin strips and add to the bowl. With both hands rub the butter into the mix, pressing it between your thumb and fingers to help incorporate it.

Once crumbly, crack in the eggs, one by one, and mix with your hands using a clenching action. Add the lime or lemon juice and mix again. Continue to mix the dry and wet parts together until the pastry starts to become one.

Put the pastry onto a lightly floured surface and knead. Do this by folding over one edge of the pastry into the middle and pressing down with the ball of your hand. Keep your hands and the work surface lightly floured. Repeat this kneading action until the pastry forms a consistent ball. This should take roughly 2 minutes. When kneading the pastry, add a little more flour until it is not sticky and forms a neat ball. *Try not to overwork the pastry—this will prevent it becoming tough and keep it crisp and cookie-like.*

Wrap tightly in plastic wrap and place in the fridge for at least 4 hours or overnight. If you want to use the pastry immediately, place it in the freezer for 30–45 minutes.

When the main course is done, rather than moving on to dessert, we often prefer to have a break and revisit the main. However, fruit following a meal is something we can't get enough of.

The edible fruit bowl is a fun way to eat—it looks spectacular, encourages sharing, and because of the sculptural pastry, there's no need for tableware. It is similar to a good cheeseboard in the way that it should be eaten. You can pick at the fruit and break off pastry with your hands as conversation continues.

We have two suggested fillings for the pastry bowl. You can make both, choose between them when the fruits are in season, or make up your own, using fruits you prefer. Roasting slices of mango creates a slightly chewier and richer treat suitable for a winter's dinner, while the fresh fruit and berries are bright, juicy, and refreshing.

EDIBLE FRUIT BOWL

Serves 4

Preparation time: 20 minutes (plus time taken to make pastry)

Cooking time: 90 minutes

10 ounces sweet pastry per bowl (see page 222)

1 tablespoon butter, for greasing

For the winter filling

5 figs

7 ounces fresh tamarind pods

10 dates

2 dried mangoes (see page 303)

For the summer filling

¾ pound strawberries

½ a pomegranate

¾ pound raspberries

7 ounces blueberries

Make your pastry dough and chill it (see page 222). Preheat the oven to 350°F. Butter an 8-inch ovenproof Pyrex bowl.

Push the pastry into a ball with your hands, then flour a clean surface and roll it out into a round ⅛ inch thick. Lift the pastry into the Pyrex bowl, making sure that the middle of the pastry is roughly in the center of the bowl. Starting from the bottom and working upward, press the pastry into the bowl, trying not to overlap it too much. The pastry should reach past the top of the bowl and slightly hang over.

With your hands, press out any differences in the thickness of the pastry. Trim any pastry that hangs more than ⅓ inch over the edge of the bowl. *Letting a little pastry hang over the edge helps to keep the pastry in place and also protects the area that will later become the final edge from getting burned.*

Pierce the pastry with a fork. *This helps air bubbles to escape and stops the pastry warping and lifting away from the bowl.* Line the inside of the pastry with foil and fill with pie weights. Let the foil hang over the edge of the pastry bowl so that the edge does not burn.

Place in the oven for 40 minutes. After 30 minutes, remove the pie weights and foil and put the pastry back into the oven for 10 more minutes. *The pastry should cook throughout and not be soft at the bottom. The top of the pastry will be crisp and it is normal for any overhanging pastry to overcook slightly.*

Once the pastry is golden brown and cooked fully, remove from the oven and leave to cool.

Once cool, trim off the overhanging pastry with a sharp knife, using a horizontal chopping action. Use the bowl as a guide for the knife to cut a clean edge around the top of the bowl. Remove the pastry from the bowl.

Chop the fruit for the fillings as you wish and put them into the pastry bowl so that each component is visible, and serve.

menu

"We got to Dover and felt like we were doing something illegal. Are you allowed to take yam over the border?"

Duval and Jacob arrived early doors, and the Mini was full to the brim. I had a heavy load to add to the wagon. We had to make it fit somehow. As I brought out bag after bag, Duval's face said a thousand words. There definitely wasn't enough room, and something had to give. In a bizarre, impetuous moment, Jacob decided it was the soccer ball that we had to sacrifice. In haste, we drove off, regretting the call massively.

We got to Dover and felt like we were doing something illegal. Are you allowed to take yam over the border? Who knows. We disembarked from the ferry and into the familiar town of Calais. Duval put his foot down and got us to Paris in good time.

It was Tuesday and our dinners were set for Thursday and Friday. Staying in Belleville, we were amazed by the market. It was the biggest, most abundant one that we'd ever seen. We got down there and enjoyed the ridiculous array of produce, especially excited by the variety of tomatoes. Then we stashed our food at the apartment and went back for round two. In the market we met a stall owner who challenged us to a game of soccer. We were all talking the talk, but unfortunately it wasn't to be. That's one of the best matches that never happened. Inspired, we found a sports shop and bought a brand new Champions League ball. It made the trip. On every side road we busted out some impromptu keep-ups to keep the spirits high.

Out of their working hours, we familiarized ourselves with Le Bal café. Anna, Alice, and Anselm had offered us the opportunity to take over the restaurant for a couple of nights, curious, I think, about how we did things. Le Bal has a series of large, public rooms scattered with small, hidden ones. The kitchen and the cellar were two such spaces that we'd spend time shuttling between. Up. Then down.

Then up again, ready for the dinner. We arrived just after their afternoon service and started our preparations. On the special occasion it was nice that my sister Lola and co. were joining us later, and to have some familiar faces behind the scenes. Our friend Hafssa came all the way from Brussels to lend a helping hand, and with an hour or two to spare she made some smooth suggestions. After I poured out the first couple she insisted that "an aperitif is to whet the palate, not get them drunk, Yemi." Ibiye took control of the front of house as we rushed around the kitchen, feeling behind. Our guests slowly funneled in, picked up a cocktail, and then headed outside for the last of the evening sun.

Just before dinner there was one last thing. We had to be introduced to our new Parisian audience. Anselm massaged our egos with the best speech known to man. We felt like boxers, on their way out before a big prizefight. Jacob called on some of his finest French. Duval put that A level into practice.

And all I could muster was "*Merci*."

I knew watermelon and ginger paired well and remembered turmeric's earthy, citrusy notes from the injera menu a few months before, so I bought some, with a hunch it would work well in this.

WATERMELON, GINGER & TURMERIC

Makes 10 drinks

Time: 10 minutes

1 small watermelon (around 6½ pounds unpeeled)

1 ounce fresh ginger (peeled weight)

¾ ounce fresh turmeric

Halve the watermelon, then hold it over a bowl as you remove the seeds to retain as much juice as possible. *Reserve the seeds; they can be roasted as a snack.*

Peel the ginger and turmeric and blend in a blender or food processor with the watermelon, then pass through a fine-mesh sieve before serving.

The technique is stolen from the moin-moin.

LIMA BEAN TERRINE

Serves 6–8

**Time: 3 hours 40 minutes
(plus 12 hours soaking)**

About 10 ounces dried lima beans

3 medium yellow bell peppers

1 fennel bulb

1 tablespoon balsamic vinegar

1 tablespoon lemon juice

1 teaspoon fine sea salt

1 teaspoon garlic powder

1 tablespoon olive oil

Soak the lima beans for at least 12 hours in plenty of fresh water. Drain them, then rinse and remove the skins. If you rub a handful of the beans with your palms facing each other, the skins should come off quite easily.

Preheat the oven to 395°F. Halve the peppers and remove the stems and seeds. Roast in the oven for 30 minutes, turning them after 15 minutes. The peppers will char slightly and the skin will begin to come away from the flesh when they're ready. Slide them into a large bowl, cover with plastic wrap, and leave to cool for 10 minutes, then remove the skins, which should come off quite easily.

To make the terrine, turn the oven down to 350°F. Roughly pulse the lima beans. Remove the outer layer of the fennel if it is tough, then trim the bulb and roughly chop. Mix all the ingredients (apart from the oil), then pulse in a blender. Add the oil and blend further. *It should be a smooth silky paste.*

Oil two 1-pound loaf pans and add the lima bean mixture to them. Cut a rectangle of foil large enough to cover the pan and oil the shiny side. Wrap it tightly to form a lid, with the shiny side facing down. *This reflects and retains the heat.* Wrap again, both sides and lengthwise, to ensure an even temperature while the terrine is steaming.

Place the loaf pan in a deep roasting pan and pour in warm water until it reaches halfway up the sides of the loaf pan. Bake on the middle rack of the oven for 2 hours.

Remove from the oven, but leave the loaf pan in the roasting pan of water for another 30 minutes. Then take it out of the water and let it rest for another 10 minutes.

Use a bread knife to separate the terrine from the sides of the pan. Invert, then shake gently to release completely. *It should slide out quite easily.*

Slice into ¾-inch-thick portions and serve at room temperature.

Kachumbari is such a versatile side dish that I think of it as a condiment, ideal to have adorning tables, as it goes with any number of meals and dishes. Often after a night out in Nairobi I visit the little roadside vendors who push around small carts with rudimentary sausage and egg cooking instruments. Halving eggs or sausages, they spoon a couple of portions of kachumbari in the middle and charge a few bob. It varies in makeup but it has a few key ingredients—red onion, tomatoes, salt, and green chile. I like it sharp and with a prominent flavor, but not too spicy. I prefer to use it liberally as a milder accompaniment. It's moreish.

KACHUMBARI

Serves 4

Time: 10 minutes

1 small green chile

½ a red onion

½ teaspoon sea salt flakes

½ pound ripe tomatoes

1 tablespoon white
wine vinegar

1 tablespoon olive oil (optional)

Halve, finely dice, then lightly crush the green chile. Put into a bowl.

Finely dice the red onion and add to the chile. Add the salt and mix.

Dice the tomatoes and add to the bowl.

Add the white wine vinegar and the olive oil, if desired, toss well, and serve.

I became fond of endives while living in Paris. They were alluring in the markets and I loved how crunchy and bitter they were. The dates make for a bittersweet salad and the dressing marries the two perfectly.

ENDIVE & DATE WITH MUSTARD TAHINI DRESSING

Serves 4

Time: 10 minutes

2 Belgian endives

4 dates, pitted

1 teaspoon English mustard

1 teaspoon tahini

1 teaspoon honey

juice of 1 lemon

½ teaspoon fine sea salt

¼ cup olive oil

Wash and halve the endive, removing any blemished areas. Remove the triangular core at the base and separate the leaves.

Chop the dates into small cubes by halving, cutting into strips, and dicing. *Working with wet hands prevents the dates from sticking.*

Mix the mustard, tahini, honey, lemon juice, and salt in a small bowl. Gradually add the olive oil, stirring as you go until it is well combined. Add more oil or a little water if a thinner dressing is desired.

Toss the dates and endive with 3 or 4 tablespoons of dressing and serve.

Sukuma wiki is a dish of greens often served with Kenyan meals. Its preparation will vary hugely depending on who is serving it. One cook might add tomatoes to the greens. Another might go for herbs or spices to dress it up. I believe that it's best prepared simply, allowing the distinctive flavor of the leaves to shine through.

When I tried to replicate this dish for Yemi and Duval I used spinach, and then kale, each of which gave its own attribute to this simple dish, yet neither tasted like what I was used to eating in Kenya. The leaves that we seek in the market are either efo tete, callaloo, or collard greens, but most greens that you find in the market will work. The leaves should give the final dish an earthy but fantastically rich, rounded flavor.

SUKUMA WIKI

Serves 4

Time: 10 minutes

1 bunch of callaloo, efo tete, collard greens, or another green of your choice

2 cloves of garlic

2 onions

2 tablespoons sunflower oil

¼ teaspoon salt

2 tablespoons vegetable stock

Wash and drain the greens and roughly chop them into strips approximately ¼ inch wide. Set aside.

Finely slice the garlic and dice the onions, then cook them with the sunflower oil over medium heat for 5 minutes, stirring frequently. Add the salt and the greens. Stir and cook for another 5 minutes over medium heat, then reduce the heat, add the stock, and leave to cook for 5 minutes more.

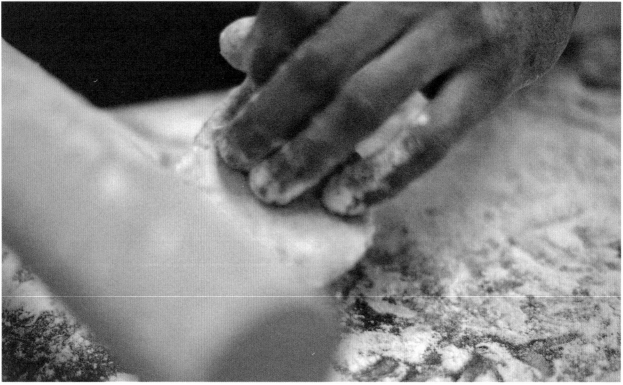

For a couple of days after the dinner, I stayed in the space while I slowly finished off the cleaning. During that period, I couldn't stop making flatbreads and eating them with shito and whatever else I had on hand in the kitchen. Since then, I've continued making flatbreads, perfecting the technique and adding other ingredients. Adding ripe plantain works well because it is sweet and gives a comforting softness that complements the rustic texture and warmth of the fresh roti.

PLANTAIN ROTI

Makes 10 small flatbreads

Time: 30 minutes

1 black plantain

generous ¾ cup water

scant 2½ cups all-purpose flour, plus extra for rolling

1 teaspoon salt

Bring a pan of water to a boil. Top and tail the plantain, then make a cut in the skin, down its length. Boil the plantain in its skin for 10 minutes, then drain and leave for a minute to cool before peeling.

In a blender or food processor, blend the plantain with the water, adding the water gradually and blending after each addition until you have used all of it and the mixture is smooth. Put the flour and salt into a bowl, add the blended plantain and mix into a dough.

On a clean floured surface, knead the dough for 4 minutes. If necessary, knead in more flour until the dough becomes dry enough to roll. With a floured rolling pin or glass bottle, roll out golfball-size (2-ounce) balls of the dough into ⅛-inch-thick discs. *It's okay if they are not perfectly circular, each one should develop its own unique character.*

Heat a frying pan to medium. Place a flatbread in the frying pan and cover. If you don't have a lid for the pan you are using, you can cover it with another pan—*this keeps some moisture in the air around the flatbread and helps pockets of air to rise inside the bread.*

After 40 seconds, flip the flatbread and cover the pan again. After another 40 seconds, remove the flatbread from the pan. Air pockets should have developed within the bread and the surface on each side should be golden brown in parts. The tip of each air pocket may char slightly, which will give the bread a light smoky flavor.

Repeat the process for each flatbread. If flour collects in the pan, wipe it off with a piece of dry paper towel to prevent it from burning.

There are few foods that are eaten throughout Kenya—on the coast, in the highlands, the lowlands, the north, south, east, west. Nyama choma is one. Then again, it is simply roasted meat, and mbuzi is a favorite. A whole leg, the shoulder, or an entire side of ribs are the preferred cuts. In Nairobi bars and restaurants there are often mini butcheries on site where goats are hung and butchered. Goat meat is lean, and it generally has less fat, calories, cholesterol, and marbling than similar red meats like beef and lamb. The paucity of fat means that if cooked quickly it risks losing moisture and drying out. A quick rub with salt and herbs—say, rosemary—might be in order, although custom requires no prepreparation.

The very first thing is that the meat is placed on a high-heat grill to sear the entire surface, browning the meat. Grills common to Nairobi have a chain-operated grate platform over a charcoal pit. To sear, the grill is kept low and the meat is turned regularly until it has a golden-brown look. Techniques vary at this point. Nevertheless the aim is then to cook the meat slowly. A distinguished art. And like many arts it requires practice, refined technique, and, above all, patience. Lots of it.

The large cooked piece of meat lifted directly from the fire should glisten deliciously. It is put on a wooden board and chopped roughly with a large sharp knife. The outside should be alluringly browned, and once first cut the clear juices will seep out over the board. The meat should be tender, with some bite. You cannot completely remove traces of the animal's lean, roaming lifestyle, nor would you want to.

The meat is carved into small, irregular pieces, with the bones and fat included on the platter. It is habitually served—at the very minimum—with ugali, pounded white corn cooked with water until it forms a hard dough, and kachumbari, a tomato, onion, and green chile salsa (see page 238).

Also with salt—a little pile of it on the side of the serving tray— to dip the meat into between mouthfuls of conversation.

NYAMA CHOMA

Serves 6

**Time: 2 hours 5 minutes
(plus resting time)**

3 handfuls sea salt flakes

3½ to 4½ pounds bone-in
goat or lamb shoulder
(or alternative cut, e.g., leg)

Take a handful of salt at a time and rub it forcefully all over the goat, ensuring that you push it into the crevices. Leave for a few minutes for the salt to settle.

Place the meat on a hot grill and turn frequently until the outside is a crisp golden brown.

Once the skin is cooked to the desired color, remove the meat from the heat and wrap repeatedly in foil. It is important that the entire piece be extremely well sealed in order that the juices do not escape. *This also helps to regulate the heat, as the moisture and foil protect the meat from direct heat.*

Return the meat to the coolest part of the grill or, if possible, raise the grates. Leave uncovered for 1½ hours to cook.

When done, remove and leave to rest for 10 minutes in a large rimmed baking sheet or container. In the meantime, get a large carving board and a good carving knife ready.

Carefully remove the foil from the meat, being aware that there may be juices trying to escape. Once the foil has been removed, transfer the meat to the carving board. First remove the meat from the bone in large pieces. Then carve these into bite-size pieces.

Place all the meat on a cutting board and serve with a pile of salt and kachambari. It needs to be served immediately—*if left for any length of time uncovered, the meat will begin to dry out.*

PERI-PERI CHICKEN

Serves 4

Time: 55 minutes (plus marinating time)

1 small whole chicken (about 1½ pounds), or 4 drumsticks and 4 thighs

4 small green chiles or African bird's-eye chiles

1 tablespoon paprika

5 cloves of garlic

1 tablespoon salt

scant ½ cup lime juice

1 tablespoon honey

1 teaspoon ground white pepper

2 tablespoons olive oil

Either ask a butcher to remove the backbone and neck of the chicken (but not the skin), or use a sharp knife or some scissors to do it yourself. We like to butterfly the breast as well, using a sharp knife to slice the breasts in two but making sure they are still attached. *This ensures that there is a greater surface area for the marinade to be in direct contact with the grill, and the overall cooking time is reduced.*

Seed 2 of the chiles and put them into a blender or a pestle and mortar with the remaining whole chiles, paprika, peeled garlic cloves, salt, lime juice, honey, and white pepper. Crush to a fine paste and set aside.

Lay the chicken on a work surface and press down on the breasts to lay it flat (so it spreads like a butterfly). Place in a container suitable for marinating, add the chile marinade and massage well into all the crevices. Leave the chicken to marinate for at least 4 hours—preferably overnight to get better flavor. *Marinating in this instance makes a real difference.*

Take the chicken out of the marinade and lay it on a grill tray under a hot broiler for 40 minutes, turning and rotating the pan every 10 minutes. Pour the remaining marinade into a bowl and add 1 tablespoon of oil. Use this sauce to coat the chicken once on each side with a pastry brush, before turning it a second time. The time it takes to cook will vary depending on the effectiveness of your broiler and the size of the chicken.

Broiling can be challenging and requires regular attention, so alternatively sear the two sides of the chicken under a hot broiler until the skin crisps, then put it into the oven at 340°F for 40 minutes.

Mandazi are East African spiced doughnuts or dumplings. They are often served with chai in the mornings or at other breaks during the day. This recipe derives from Kenya—the coconut milk and spices are very common up the Swahili coast, which differentiates the dough from West African versions, like the Nigerian puff-puff, which typically omits these flavors. It pairs well with kunnu and our pineapple jam (see pages 254 and 257).

MANDAZI

Makes approximately 25 small doughnuts

Time: 50 minutes (plus 1 hour resting time)

2 teaspoons active dry yeast

½ cup plus 2 tablespoons and 1 teaspoon superfine sugar

4½ cups bread flour plus ⅓ cup for rolling

1 teaspoon ground cinnamon

1 teaspoon fine sea salt

1 teaspoon ground cardamom

1 medium egg

generous ¾ cup coconut milk

3 quarts sunflower oil, for frying

Dissolve the yeast in ½ cup of warm water and add 1 teaspoon of the superfine sugar.

In a large bowl, sift together the flour and cinnamon. Add the salt, ½ cup of sugar, and the cardamom. *To extract the best flavor from cardamom, crush whole cardamom pods, remove the seeds, and crush them with a pestle and mortar.*

In a bowl, mix together the egg, coconut milk, the rest of the sugar, and a tablespoon of oil until well combined.

Add the yeast liquid and the egg mixture to the flour and mix together, using a fork, until combined.

Dust a work surface with flour and knead the dough for 10 minutes, until it has a smooth texture that does not stick to your fingers but is slightly sticky to the touch. Cover and allow to rise for at least 1 hour in a warm place.

Heat the sunflower oil to 350°F in a deep-sided pan or a deep-fat fryer.

Shape the dough into small (table-tennis-size) balls and place them on a lightly floured flat surface. Slowly, using a slotted spoon, add the dough balls to the hot oil so they aren't cramped. They will expand slightly on cooking.

Cook for 5–10 minutes, or until they turn golden brown. It'll be necessary to turn them periodically to ensure they cook evenly. *They can be tricky to turn, as initially they lean one side up. However, with a little practice and some tongs you'll be able to turn them and get them cooked evenly.* Regulate the oil temperature to ensure that the mandazi are cooked all the way through.

Remove from the oil and place on a rack or a dish lined with paper towels. If desired, sprinkle lightly with sugar while they are still hot and just out of the fryer so that the sugar sticks.

Serve hot or at room temperature. If storing for the longer term, seal well at room temperature and reheat before serving.

I tried to shoehorn pineapple into many a menu and the boys finally let the jam slide. It's sharp, tangy, and sweet, which offsets the moreish mandazi on page 253.

Pineapples are low in pectin, so the lime juice is crucial to help the jam set. I prefer truer conical pineapples—my mum calls them Cotonou, after the large coastal city in Benin—which have a paler flesh. They taste more applelike, hence the name I guess.

PINEAPPLE JAM

Enough for 12 mandazi

Time: 1 hour

1 large pineapple
(1¾ pounds peeled weight)

3 limes

1⅓ cups demerara sugar

Top and tail the pineapple. Standing it up vertically, peel, halve, and then quarter. Make angled incisions either side of the core and remove (but don't throw it away—you can eat it as you go along!).

Over a large mixing bowl—*so you can catch the juices*—coarsely grate the flesh. You could also chop it into very small pieces—just make sure they're the same size.

Put the grated pineapple and juices into a pan and add ⅔ cup of water. Bring to a rolling boil, cover, then simmer over medium-low heat for 15 minutes. The flesh should soften considerably.

Juice the limes and add to the pan with the sugar. Stir to help the sugar dissolve. Reduce to low heat and cook for 30 minutes, uncovered, stirring every 4 minutes or so. The amount of liquid in the mixture should reduce, and when it starts to resemble jam, it's ready (if you have a thermometer the setting point is 219°F). It will thicken a little more as it cools.

Kunnu is particularly popular in northern Nigeria. It's a kind of "milk" made from grains, cereals, or nuts, which are soaked and then blended in water along with other seasonings. One of the favored variations is made with rice. Another with tiger nuts. Our kunnu is a blend of the two.

KUNNU

Serves 8

Time: 6 hours

8 ounces tiger nuts or shredded coconut

2½ cups cooked rice

20 cardamom pods

1 teaspoon salt

If you are using tiger nuts, wash them, then soak in plenty of fresh water for a minimum of 6 hours in the refrigerator. Drain, then blend in 1⅔ cups of fresh cold water. Add another 1⅔ cups of water and blend thoroughly.

If you are using shredded coconut, steep it in 3⅓ cups very hot water for a couple of minutes, then blend for 4 minutes.

Pass the liquid through a fine mesh sieve, or better still a double layer of cheesecloth. *The objective is to extract as much of the "milk" as possible.* It should yield a generous 2 cups.

Blend freshly cooked rice with 1⅔ cups fresh cold water. Add another 1⅔ cups, blend again, and then a final 1⅔ cups. Blend until the rice milk is absolutely smooth to taste. It should yield a bit over 4 cups.

Crush the cardamom pods and salt with a pestle and mortar and add to the liquid. Combine the rice milk with your tiger nut or coconut milk, mix well and refrigerate until cold.

Shake well or stir the milk before serving.

menu

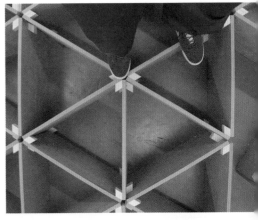

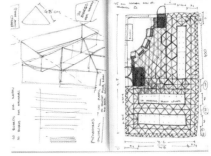

"The food never stands still and neither does the setting. Changing things keeps up our motivation."

The food never stands still and neither does the setting. Changing things keeps up our motivation. We'd been at the Arthouse in July and were heading back for a week in November. The members enjoyed having us and we liked being there. All we needed was another long table in the set. The space could comfortably fit more people and we missed the intimacy of St. John's Hall. We needed to find another way.

We discussed building benches in June, but copped out in the end. But how about making the floor into the seats, Duval asked. Then we went on, gassing about how great it'd be.

Back in the cold light of our studio we questioned how viable this was. Building a whole floor for a week of dinners was impractical, in many ways, but practicality wasn't the only reason. We decided to go for it, and once again left Duval to work wonders with Pythagoras. He'll have to interject with drawings of how it all came together, but all I remember was carrying lots of wood to and from Duval's place. During the setup, the boys busied themselves building structures, cutting wood, and stretching fabric over the "floor" while I got the shopping in. A whole lot of shopping.

I usually approach the market with an open mind, ready to be inspired by a great deal or an ingredient that looks particularly fresh. That said, if you're in the right place at the right time, pretty much anything is in season in London. Sometimes I'm more specific and go to stands with a familiar face on the other side. Never a name, just "good to see you, boss," and it's difficult to say who is employing whom since we both feed off each other.

When it comes to our events I ready myself for the short trip with a heavy list in hand, and my strategy in place. Onions. Beans. Yam. Plantain. Check. These staples come first because they live the longest, while the fresh meat and leaves come into play last, to make sure they stay that way.

At the end of the week we stood up to thank everybody for coming and were touched by the rapturous applause. It had been the most intense week I can remember. And it was time to make some speeches. Mine had been getting progressively worse over the events but in this one, I just crumbled. I started to cry. Sandro, who's been on hand helping at most of our dinners, said it felt like it was the end, like I was saying goodbye. It did, in some way, feel like the end of a chapter.

SAGE BRANDY

Makes 6 cocktails

Time: 2 hours

30 sage leaves

2¼ cups demerara sugar

10 ounces fresh sugarcane

generous 2 cups brandy

generous ¾ cup hard cider

Pick the sage leaves from the stems.

Measure out the sugar into a pan and add a generous 2 cups water. Heat over medium heat until the sugar dissolves completely. This should take around 3 minutes.

Add the sage leaves and simmer for another minute.

Remove from the heat, but leave the sage to steep in the syrup. You can use it when it has cooled completely, but the longer you leave the sage in the syrup, the more flavor it takes on.

Peel the sugarcane and slice it into straw-size strips. *You'll need a strong knife or a cleaver to get into it.*

Combine a generous ¾ cup of the sage syrup with the brandy, apple cider, and 1⅔ cups of water.

Add a sugarcane stick to each glass and serve over ice.

After a conversation with a Nigerian you'd think that peppe' had never ended in R. By peppe', they mean hot pepper; something that is known by the lyrical phrase "red hot chile pepper" in the English lexicon.

In tropical cuisines hot peppers feature heavily, and Nigeria is no exception. Peppe' soup is essentially a thin, fiery broth that has always been a popular remedy for people who are under the weather. Traditionally it is made with the offcuts and entrails of a chicken, goat, or cow. We use ese-eran, or cow foot, which is one of my personal favorites. The bone is packed with flavor while the flesh is warm and comforting, like a savory gummy bear.

Ese-eran is available from most African, Caribbean, and Asian butchers. Ask them to machine-slice it into small pieces for you.

PEPPE' SOUP

Serves 8

Time: 1 hour 15 minutes

2¼ pounds cow foot, chopped into small pieces

vinegar, for washing

2 quarts cold water

1 tablespoon salt

1 teaspoon garlic powder

1 teaspoon ground ginger

2 Scotch bonnet peppers

2½ cups vegetable stock (see page 313)

Clean the pieces of cow foot with a little vinegar and water, then rinse thoroughly.

Put them into a large deep pot and add the cold water. Bring to a boil over a high heat, then add salt to infuse the water. Leave to boil, uncovered, for 15 minutes. Remove the initial froth with a slotted spoon as it rises to the surface.

Reduce to a medium-low simmer, then add the garlic powder, ginger, and the Scotch bonnet peppers (pierced a couple of times to release the flavor). Cook, *covered,* for another 45 minutes. While this is cooking, prepare the vegetable stock if you haven't already. See page 313 for the method.

Remove a piece of cow foot to check for tenderness. *You should be able to slice the flesh through to the bone without much effort when it's ready.*

Remove all the pieces, but do not discard the liquid. Take the flesh off the bone. Chop into bite-size pieces, ready for the soup.

To make the soup, blend the cow foot broth until it starts to appear a creamy brown color. Combine the vegetable stock with the broth and pulse until melded.

Serve with a few pieces of cow foot per portion to complete the soup.

Running through the beans to pick out stones, stray rice, and corn needs patience, but is definitely necessary. It's a peaceful task to collect your thoughts, and even better with good company to lend a helping hand. Honey beans don't require soaking, so beyond selection they're a convenient pulse. And, as the name suggests, they have a special sweetness that I love.

In its entirety this recipe draws inspiration from Ghanaian red-red, a dish of black-eyed peas stewed in tomatoes, combined with red palm oil. It's a wholesome dish that can be enjoyed at any time of day.

HONEY BEAN RED-RED

Serves 4

Time: 1 hour 30 minutes

14 ounces honey or black-eye beans

3 red onions

2 tablespoons olive oil

3 cloves of garlic

2 teaspoons salt

14 ounces canned or fresh plum tomatoes

2 tablespoons tomato paste

generous ¾ cup chicken (or vegetable) stock

2 tablespoons red palm oil

Sift out any stones and stray pieces from the beans. Rinse the beans, then drain and set aside.

Finely slice the red onions and soften in 1 tablespoon of olive oil for 10 minutes over medium heat. Crush the garlic to a paste with 1 teaspoon of salt, and add to the onion. Cook for another 10 minutes.

Add the plum tomatoes, tomato paste, ½ cup of the chicken stock, and the red palm oil. Stir well. Reduce the heat to low and simmer for 15 minutes.

Put the honey beans into a large separate pot and cover with plenty of cold water. Bring to a boil, then add the other tablespoon of olive oil and 1 teaspoon salt. Leave over high heat for 10 minutes, skimming any scum that rises to the surface. Then reduce the heat and leave to simmer for 20 minutes, until the beans are cooked but still have a firm texture.

Drain the parboiled honey beans and add to the tomato mixture with the remaining ¼ cup chicken stock. Simmer together for another 15 minutes so the flavors meld.

This recipe warms the heart of my big sister, Omolola. She insists that she can't make it like I can, but I reckon she just likes being pampered once in a while. Don't we all. Yam can be a little dry on its own but this mash is silky smooth, with the coconut giving it a richness. The most effective way to store excess yam is to peel the tubers, slice into discs, and freeze it in portions. You can boil it from frozen when you're ready to use it.

YAM & PLANTAIN SCOOP

Serves 6

Time: 30 minutes

1 pound puna yam

1 black plantain

2 tablespoons extra virgin coconut oil

1 teaspoon ground white pepper

1 teaspoon fine sea salt

Peel the yam, removing all the dark outer bark. *Some tubers have woody bark running to the core in some areas. Remove it, preserving as much flesh as possible.* Slice the yam into ¾-inch discs, halve, then quarter. Put in a pot and cover with cold water. Bring to a boil and simmer for 8 minutes.

Top and tail the plantain, then make a skin-deep incision along the spine. Peel and cut into 4 even pieces, crosswise. Add to the pan of simmering yam and leave for another 8 minutes. *Add a little more warm water if the plantain and yam are not sufficiently covered.*

In the meantime, measure out the coconut oil and seasoning.

Check if the yam is done by removing a piece and inserting a fork. *If you can do so with relative ease, it's ready.* Yam is robust and can withstand "overcooking," so don't worry if any pieces have boiled inconsistently.

Check the plantain by removing one piece and halving it crosswise on a cutting board. *You want each piece to be the same bright yellow as the outside through the cross section.*

When both yam and plantain are ready, drain in a colander and return them to the dry pan. Working quickly, add the coconut oil and mash thoroughly while hot. It usually takes 2–3 minutes to achieve a smooth consistency. Season with the salt and white pepper and mash one last time. I like to use a fork for this part.

Ball with an ice cream scoop and serve immediately.

CUCUMBER & RADISH

To make a salad for 4 to 6, peel a daikon (white radish or mooli). Chop up the daikon,
one cucumber, and a handful of red radishes into strips roughly ⅛ inch wide and up to 4 inches long.
Toss all of the components and serve as fresh as possible.

Guinea fowl is a common bird, native to West Africa. Often served in stews,
it is used interchangeably with chicken, identifiable when raw by its dark flesh.

TOMATO STEW WITH GUINEA FOWL

Serves 4

Time: 2 hours 25 minutes

2 tablespoons peanut oil

1 guinea fowl (about 2½ pounds),
skin removed, chopped
into 8 chunks

6 tomatoes

2 onions

1 red bell pepper, seeded

2 tablespoons tomato paste

scant ½ cup chicken stock

1 Scotch bonnet pepper

1 tablespoon salt

2 tablespoons red palm oil

Heat the peanut oil in a large pan and brown the guinea fowl over medium to high heat. Once the guinea fowl has taken on a light brown color on all sides, remove it from the pan, leaving the oil behind. Put it into a dish and cover.

Blend the tomatoes in a food processor. It is a good idea to chop them roughly first. Add the blended tomatoes to the oil in the pan and cook over medium-high heat for 25 minutes, stirring occasionally, until they start to dry out—there should be air pockets releasing small bubbles of air. In the meantime, blend the onions and bell pepper in the processor, chopping into chunks first. After 25 minutes add the tomato paste and the blended red pepper and onion mix and cook for another 25 minutes, stirring occasionally.

Turn the heat down to low. Add the chicken stock, Scotch bonnet pepper (pierce a couple of times to release the flavor), salt, and guinea fowl and stir well. After 20 minutes, add the palm oil, cook for another 10 minutes, then turn off the heat. Allow to rest for 15 minutes before serving.

Legend says it's called Palava because people fuss and fight over it, and my mum and dad are no exception. Whenever it's mentioned, their faces light up and the room fills with enthusiastic stories about how much they love the dish, as if they were telling us for the first time. The sauce has been a big talking point for us as it's one of the dishes that tastes distinctly West African, with its reliance on smoked fish with bitter and fresh leaves, underpinned by onions and palm oil. Our recipe only calls for fish, although it's commonly made with meat as well. Auntie Ellen insists that it's best when you "bang it all in" one pot, and the final sauce is typically served with plain rice.

Cassava leaves, which form the foundation of the dish, can be found in African and Asian stores (often prepounded and frozen). However, if you can't get hold of either, spinach is a great substitute.

PALAVA SAUCE

Serves 6

Time: 1 hour 40 minutes

2 quarts water

2 teaspoons salt

1 teaspoon black pepper

2¼ pounds fresh fish (e.g., mackerel; barracuda; sea bream, porgy, or dorade), scaled, gutted, and cleaned

9 ounces cassava leaves or finely chopped spinach leaves

1 Scotch bonnet pepper

1¼ pounds onions

3 cloves of garlic

2 ounces fresh ginger

1½ ounces smoked dried shrimp, finely blended

2 tablespoons tomato paste

2 tablespoons tahini or smooth peanut butter

3 tablespoons red palm oil

Bring the water, salt, and black pepper to a boil in a large pan. Add the fish and let it cook for about 10 minutes. Once the fish is cooked through, carefully remove it from the liquid and let it rest for a few minutes. This resting time allows the flesh to firm up and prevents it falling apart.

With your hands, gently remove the skin of the fish and take the flesh off the bones, trying to keep the pieces as large as possible. Set the chunks of fish aside. Blend the cassava leaves into small pieces in a blender or using a pestle and mortar.

Bring the liquid in the pan back to a boil. Pierce the Scotch bonnet, add it to the pan with the blended leaves, and simmer for 10 minutes. (If you are using spinach, do not add it yet.)

Finely slice the onions, garlic, and ginger and add them to the pan. Leave to simmer for 50 minutes, stirring occasionally, then add the smoked dried shrimp, tomato paste, and tahini and simmer for another 10 minutes.

Add the palm oil and the cooked fish. If you're using spinach, add it to the pot now. Leave the sauce to cook gently for another 5 minutes. Serve hot with plain white rice.

SESAME & ALMOND SNAP

Makes one 12-inch snap

Time: 25 minutes

⅔ cup sesame seeds

½ teaspoon salt

3½ ounces raw almonds

½ cup demerara sugar

½ teaspoon grated fresh ginger

3½ tablespoons water

sugar thermometer

Place the sesame seeds and salt in a shallow frying pan and dry-fry them over medium heat for a few minutes, until the seeds are golden brown. Shake or stir the pan regularly so that the seeds brown evenly. Add the almonds and set aside.

Cut off two 16-inch lengths of wax paper and lay on a flat surface. Have a rolling pin ready nearby.

Put the sugar, grated ginger, and water into a small narrow pan and bring to a boil, stirring briefly to ensure that the sugar is fully dissolved. The sugar should quickly melt, begin to bubble, and reduce slowly. Measure the temperature with a thermometer until it reaches 320°F, by which time the melted sugar will have become a dark brown color.

As soon as the sugar reaches this temperature, take the pan off the heat, add the sesame seeds and almonds, and stir. Work quickly to combine the mix, then quickly pour the hot mix into the middle of the first sheet of wax paper and cover it with the second sheet. With the rolling pin, quickly roll out the mix so that it forms a big flat disc between the two layers of paper. Be forceful with the rolling pin so that you create a disc that is as thin as possible. The mix will solidify very quickly as it cools, so it is important to work fast.

Leave the disc to cool for 10 minutes, then peel away the paper. Snap the disc into shareable-size pieces with your hands before eating. The snaps can be stored in an airtight container for up to a week.

Fruit pastilles are something we all have a soft spot for; who doesn't love one as a cheeky sweetener alongside the bill come the end of a meal? With a sweet treat in mind, we worked on developing a little something that would cap the night off in style for our guests.

Our pastille is comparable to many cornstarch-based treats from across the world, while the pink peppercorns were inspired by a trip to visit our friend Sarah's family home in the sleepy village of Aniane. They look and taste intriguing. Kind of sweet, and somewhat floral.

PINK PEPPERCORN PASTILLE

Serves 4

Time: 4 hours 30 minutes

3 tablespoons pink peppercorns

2¼ cups granulated sugar

juice of 1 lemon

candy thermometer

½ cup plus 4 teaspoons cornstarch

1 teaspoon cream of tartar

Line the bottom of an 8-inch-square baking pan with parchment paper.

Lightly crush the pink peppercorns and set aside.

Put the sugar into a heavy-bottomed pot with the lemon juice and a generous ¾ cup of water. Place over medium heat. Bring to a boil and heat until it reaches 241°F on a sugar thermometer. It will take at least 5 minutes once it comes to a boil.

At the same time, put the cornstarch and cream of tartar into a separate pan with 1½ cups of water. Whisk well. *Don't worry if it seems stiff. It loosens up with a good stir.* Place over medium heat and cook until the mixture has thickened. It should take about 8 minutes.

When the sugar and water mixture has reached 241°F, add the cornstarch mixture and whisk vigorously to combine. Return to low heat and cook for 20–30 minutes, until thickened and light golden brown.

Remove from the heat and carefully pour into the lined baking pan. Sprinkle the peppercorns evenly over the pastille before it fully sets.

Slice into individual pieces to serve.

Keep in the refrigerator to maintain freshness.

Hibiscus drinks are prepared in a variety of ways: cold-filtered, hot, or blended with other leaves or roots. The petals are a distinctive reddish-purple and lend their color to the drink once submerged in water. The dry, compact flowers will absorb water, expand, and unfurl, leaving vivid-colored matter that resembles seaweed in your strainer. Hibiscus has a sharp citruslike flavor and tastes very cleansing, so you might believe the purported medicinal benefits that some vendors peddle you along with the flowers.

HIBISCUS TEA

Serves 1

Time: 5 minutes

1 heaping tablespoon
hibiscus flowers

1 teaspoon granulated sugar
(optional)

To prepare, put the hibiscus flowers into a mug. Pour in about 1 cup of boiling water and leave to rest for 3 minutes. Strain the flowers through a tea strainer, add the sugar to taste, if desired, and serve.

bru

nch

Tinned food is common in our households, and while in the main we attempt to stay away from processed and packaged food, somehow the convenience and longevity of cans means that they are always on hand, which is useful when trying to prepare something quickly. There is a lot of flexibility with this recipe, and any number of canned fishes work—Yemi favors sardines or mackerel, and I love anchovies. Duval disagrees with eggs generally so he usually misses out on this conversation.

ANCHOVY OMELETTE

Makes 1 omelette

Time: 25 minutes

1 onion

½ a green bell pepper

2 tablespoons sunflower oil

1 teaspoon berbere spice blend

1 teaspoon ras el hanout

4 cherry tomatoes

3 eggs

One 2-ounce (56g) can of anchovies or 4.4-ounce (125g) can of mackerel sardines

Dice the onion and finely slice the green pepper and put them into a frying pan with the sunflower oil. Cook over medium heat for 5 minutes, until the onion starts to brown slightly and caramelize.

Add the spices and mix well. Halve the cherry tomatoes and add to the pan, then continue cooking, stirring often, for another 5 minutes.

In a bowl, whisk the eggs well. Open the canned fish.

Make sure the cooked vegetables are evenly distributed around the pan, then pour in the eggs and leave for a couple of minutes. Place the anchovy fillets tactically around the pan. As the fillets cook the eggs should start to set in place.

Turn the heat down to low and cook for another 5 minutes, or until the top of the omelette has begun to set. Carefully run a spatula under the omelette to lift it up, and slide it onto a plate.

Serve hot.

Ful mesdames is a dish made from fava beans, often topped with chopped onion, herbs, tomatoes, hard-boiled eggs, and cheese and usually accompanied by some bread. It is eaten for breakfast, lunch, or dinner in Egypt, Sudan, and South Sudan and further afield. A former colleague of mine, Kit, used to make it with an assortment of other salads and dishes for communal lunches at work, which borrowed much from his experience of Sudanese meals. It is always served in a bowl to be shared. I loved these meals.

In Sudan, dried fava beans are frequently cooked overnight over extremely low heat in a purpose-made pot. However, I most often tend to cheat and use canned beans, because they are tasty and take far less time than the 2 hours minimum that is required to cook dried fava beans properly. I also love the retro red, yellow, and blue cans of one brand of ful on my shelves, the sight of which pleases me almost as much as the content.

FUL MESDAMES

Serves 2–4

Time: 3 hours 10 minutes

9 ounces dried fava beans or one 14-ounce can of ful mesdames

1 teaspoon salt (if using dried beans)

1 large tomato

¼ of a red onion

1 egg (optional)

2 tablespoons sesame oil

1 teaspoon ground cumin

If using dried beans, soak the beans overnight in 1 quart of water. Drain the beans and wash them, then put them into a deep pan with 3 cups of water. Turn the heat to medium-low and cook for 3 hours. Add the salt and stir, mashing some of the beans.

If using canned beans, open the can and drain off a quarter of the liquid. Put the beans into a shallow pan over medium heat for 5 minutes, stirring regularly. Mash some of the beans in the pan and continue to stir for another 2 minutes.

Finely chop the tomato and very finely dice the onion and set both aside. If using the egg, put it into boiling water for 7 minutes, then remove and peel.

Pour the hot beans into a bowl and sprinkle the diced onion and tomato on top. Pour over the sesame oil and sprinkle with the cumin.

Halve (or quarter) the boiled egg (if using) and place on top, then serve.

Feel for an avocado that yields a little when you squeeze it gently, but does not feel too soft under the skin, if you want to eat it immediately. A hard avocado should still be fine but will need a couple of days to ripen nicely.

In the market you can politely ask the vendor to open one so you can inspect the inside; the flesh should range from a pale green to a creamy yellow color without any brown or black blemishes. If you visit a certain stand often, you'll build rapport with the vendor and trust in the quality of their produce.

There are many varieties but the most abundant are the Hass—with the dark, thick knobby skin—and variants of the smooth green. Avocados with thin skin can be eaten without peeling them if you wish.

AVOCADO

Slice through the avocado from the top downward until your knife hits the pit. Continue to rotate the knife around the pit until you have worked your way all around the fruit. Twist the two sides in different directions so that they come apart. Ease the pit out with a knife. Cut the avocado again lengthwise or scoop the flesh out with a spoon and serve.

The idea for this recipe came from Jacob's excitement about the diversity and quality of tomatoes that you can find in the markets around Paris. We handpicked tomatoes from different market stands, finding exciting shapes, colors, and flavors. While we were at it, we found some gorgeous green plums and decided to throw in a few as false tomatoes, which works as a nice surprise.

TOMATO & PLUM

Serves 4

Time: 4 minutes

1 lemon

1 lime

10 ounces tomatoes

4 ounces plums

1 teaspoon olive oil

a pinch of sea salt flakes

Zest the lemon and lime.

Slice the tomatoes into wedges or ⅓-inch-thick slices, depending on size and shape. If the tomatoes have a particularly knobbly form, slicing them into cross sections is a nice way to show them off.

Halve the plums, remove the pits, and halve them again.

Toss the tomatoes and plums with the olive oil and the citrus zest.

Sprinkle with the sea salt and serve.

This fresh red grape juice is really simple and worth making because the flavor is so superior to anything you can buy. It will blow you away!

RED GRAPE JUICE

To make a pitcher of the juice, put 2¼ pounds of red or black grapes in a blender with a generous 1 cup of cold water and blend until it forms a fine liquid. Then pass the juice through a coarse sieve or strainer to remove any last bits before serving.

As well as being used in our granola and edible fruit bowl recipes, dried mango makes the perfect sweet and chewy snack. The best way to make it is to leave the mango slices out in a hot sunny area or to use a food dehydrator, but if neither of those options are available to you, you can make them in the oven. It takes some time—however, it is easy to do, there's no extra sugar necessary and if you dry lots of mangoes, the process is more than worthwhile.

DRIED MANGO

Serves 6

Time: 6 hours

4 mangoes

Preheat a convection oven to 125°F or use a food dehydrator.

Peel the mangoes. Cut the flesh into ⅓-inch-thick slices and discard the pit (sucking the remaining flesh of the pit is a great on-the-job snack).

Place the mango slices on a baking sheet (or sheets) lined with parchment paper. Place them in the oven for 6 hours, flipping the slices every hour.

When the mango slices have shriveled up and are dry and chewy, they are ready. There shouldn't be any moist flesh, and the longer you leave them the better they will be.

Leave the slices to cool, then place them in a sealed container. They will keep for up to a week.

This granola is the foundation of my perfect breakfast. The cardamom, ginger, and bay leaves create an aroma that wakes up the senses. Garri works well in this because the crushed, dried, and roasted cassava granules lend their dry texture to the mix. Each batch of golden clusters nestled against chewy slices of dried fruit will last up to a week.

GRANOLA

Serves 6

Time: 1 hour

1 ounce fresh ginger

20 cardamom pods

3½ ounces egusi seeds

3½ ounces almonds

1 cup garri

1¼ cups rolled oats

scant 3 tablespoons sunflower oil

1¼ cups honey

juice of ½ a lemon

6 fresh bay leaves (optional)

5 ounces dried mango
(see page 303)

Preheat the oven to 395°F.

Peel the ginger and cut the flesh into tiny cubes.

Crush the cardamom pods using a pestle and mortar, and discard the papery green shell of the pods so that you are left with just the black seeds. Add the chopped ginger to the cardamom seeds in the mortar and crush to a paste with the pestle.

Mix all the ingredients (except the dried mango) in a large bowl. Once the ingredients are well mixed, roughly squeeze the mixture with your hands so that it forms clumps.

Pour the mixture on to a baking sheet and place in the oven for 45 minutes. Turn the mixture every 10 minutes so that the granola cooks evenly until it is golden brown and crunchy.

Leave the mixture to cool, then add the dried mango and remove the bay leaves if you used them.

Once cool, store the granola in a sealed container in a cool, dry place. It will keep for a week.

Serve the granola with plain yogurt, milk, or kunnu.

Whenever we are lucky enough to be in Freetown, each member of the family rolls out from under their respective mosquito net and strolls onto the balcony to watch the view of the landscape emerge as the sun rises and the mist clears. Being a fan of sleeping, I'm usually the last to arrive. By then I have to hurry for the last sweet segments of paw-paw.

PAPAYA

Halve the fruit lengthwise and remove the black seeds gently with a spoon before slicing it into the desired-size pieces to share. The full flavor of papaya really appears when the musky-tasting fruit meets the acidity of freshly squeezed lime, so it's worth slicing a lime to squeeze over the papaya as you're eating.

stock

list

Homemade stock adds depth of flavor to any recipe that could otherwise be made with water, and uses those extra vegetables that sometimes get a bit sad.

Although we give our recipe below, stock is a flexible thing. You can make a great one without one or two of the ingredients below, so it's no big deal if you don't have everything on hand.

VEGETABLE STOCK

Makes 1 quart
Time: 40 minutes

4 celery stalks

4 carrots

2 leeks

4 onions

2 bulbs of garlic

1 tablespoon black peppercorns

1 tablespoon coarse crystal salt

4 bay leaves

Roughly chop the celery, carrots, and leeks. Halve the onions and cut the garlic in half through its equator.

Place the vegetables in a large deep pan and add the peppercorns, salt, and bay leaves. Add 6 cups water, to cover the vegetables.

Bring the mixture to a boil, then turn down to low heat and simmer, uncovered, for at least 30 minutes.

Strain the liquid. Decant the stock into a sterilized container and store in the fridge until ready to use.

A real chicken stock has a beautiful depth of flavor and oil content that cannot be replicated by bouillon cubes or granules. When you get used to making chicken stocks, they really only take a few minutes to get going and they look after themselves while you get on with other cooking. If you are cooking some chicken, take the skin and bones off it to create the stock. If you're not already using a chicken, we recommend buying chicken feet, neck, or wings, because they are cheap and the amount of skin and bones in these cuts will give great flavor to your stock.

You can make this stock well in advance and store it in the fridge for a couple of days once it has been strained and decanted.

CHICKEN STOCK

Makes 1 quart

Time: 50 minutes

skin and bones of 1 chicken (or 6 chicken feet or wings)

1 teaspoon olive oil (optional)

3 onions

4 carrots

2 celery stalks

2 bulbs of garlic

4 bay leaves

1 teaspoon white or black peppercorns

1 tablespoon flaky sea salt

In a deep heavy-bottomed pot, fry the chicken skin and bones in 1 teaspoon of oil over a high heat. Stir frequently for 5 minutes until browned all over. (Omit this stage if you are using the skin and bones of a cooked chicken.)

Peel and halve the onions. Wash and peel the carrots if necessary and halve them lengthwise. Halve the celery, then lightly crush the cloves from both garlic bulbs.

Add the vegetables and bay leaves to the pot and cover with 6 cups of cold water. Bring the mixture to a boil over high heat.

Add the peppercorns and salt to the stock and then reduce to a low simmer.

Cook uncovered over low heat for at least 40 minutes.

Strain the liquid. Decant the stock into a sterilized container and store in the fridge until ready to use.

Our first batch of groundnut butter was a revelation. Peeling the skins off the peanuts can be fantastically time-consuming, but it really requires no attention—I've sat many times doing it while watching a film. I'm transfixed by the blending process. It transforms the peanuts from nuts to crumble to an oily paste. The oils are gradually teased out as the paste churns into an oily ball and finally becomes peanut butter. We use it to make groundnut soups and stews, as well as using it as a spread. This recipe is purely peanuts and self-preserving.

GROUNDNUT BUTTER

Makes 1 pound

Time: 1 hour 15 minutes

1 pound shelled peanuts

Preheat the oven to 350°F.

Place on a large rimmed baking sheet. Roast on the middle rack of the oven for 15 minutes, until the nuts are golden and the red skins begin to shed.

Remove from the oven and allow to cool for 10 minutes, then shake the baking sheet and coarsely rub the nuts between the palms of your hands (or use a tea towel). Remove as much of the skin as possible before transferring the nuts to a bowl. This is the longest part of the process but can be fairly therapeutic if you find repetitive tasks soothing.

Once all the peanuts have their skins removed, put them into a blender and start blending. This will take approximately 10–15 minutes. Make sure that the blender blades are reaching the peanuts and the blender is not just on full speed for the whole time. Give the machine a rest every 5 minutes or so to allow the blades and the mixture to cool slightly.

After 10 minutes the mixture should start to resemble peanut butter, and have been blended to a smooth liquid paste.

Remove and store in a sterilized jar in a dry, cool place.

This is an easy way to elevate a humble glass of water. The colorful cubes cool the temperature of the water, enhance flavor, and look beautiful. It is worth making a big batch and keeping them in the freezer for a sunny day. Serve them in a big jug of water at the table.

FLAVORED ICE CUBES

Makes 14 ice cubes

Time: 5 minutes (plus 3 hours freezing time)

For lemon ice cubes

4 lemons

Peel the outer layer off 3 of the lemons and chop it into strips ¼ inch wide and 1¼ inches long.

Place the peel in an ice cube tray.

Halve all the lemons and squeeze their juice. Strain the juice and pour it into the ice cube tray on top of the peel.

Place in the freezer for 3 hours. When frozen, pop the ice cubes out of the ice cube tray and store in a plastic container in the freezer until ready to use.

For lime ice cubes

4 limes

Halve the limes, squeeze their juice, and pour it into an ice cube tray.

Place in the freezer for 3 hours. When frozen, pop the ice cubes out of the ice cube tray and store in a plastic container in the freezer until ready to use.

For cucumber and mint ice cubes

1 cucumber

10 sprigs of fresh mint

Roughly chop the cucumber and place it in a blender with the mint leaves.

Blend to a fine liquid, then strain the liquid and pour it into the ice cube tray.

Place in the freezer for 3 hours. When frozen, pop the ice cubes out of the ice cube tray and store in a plastic container in the freezer until ready to use.

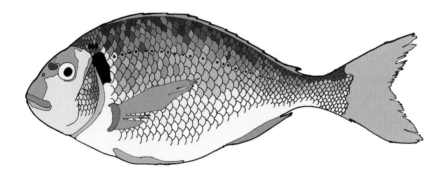

FISH

Fish is an important part of the diet across coastal regions of West Africa. Fresh fish is often seasoned well and cooked simply like we have done with our sea bream and kingfish recipes. Fish is also often smoked and/or dried, which creates a tougher texture and a deeper flavor that can be used in soups, stews, or sauces such as our shito or palava.

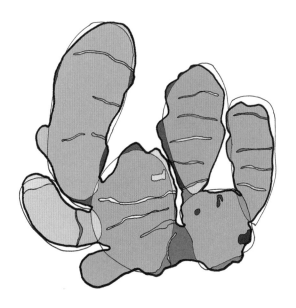

GINGER

Ginger is one of the prominent flavors in our cooking. We use it to marinade, season, garnish, to create dressings, and to make ginger beer. Small hands of ginger are often overlooked because they take more time to prepare, however they can often be more flavorful than the larger rhizomes. When peeling the skin of the ginger (which is slightly bitter and can hold dirt), use a small spoon to scrape the skin of the ginger away from the flesh instead of using a peeler or knife, because it allows you to work your way in and out of the crevices without wasting much of the beautiful flesh. Dried ginger is also important—especially in stews and sauces—because the flavor of the powder, which is musky and sharp when raw, melds well with other ingredients when given time cooking.

GROUNDNUTS

Groundnuts are peanuts by another name. In the UK, peanuts are most often seen as
a snack to have with drinks—salted, honey-, or dry-roasted. In the U.S., peanut butter rules
supreme. In Nigeria, powdered peanut coats meat in the popular snack suya. In South Sudan
okra and peanut paste are combined, and in Sierra Leone you get groundnut stew,
which changes name and recipe house by house across Africa.

In South Sudanese villages and towns there will often be one central grinder,
and villagers will take their harvest of nuts to be ground to a paste.
Groundnuts are self-preserving, protein-filled, and nutritious.

PALM OIL

The oil palm tree is a victim of its ability to thrive in both native and other tropical environments, where humans transplanted it. Originally from West Africa, it has been the fundamental cooking oil for centuries, characterizing many traditional dishes with its distinctive aroma and colorful flavor. It's an equally important component of our cooking—lending color, a smooth texture, and rich flavor—and it probably wouldn't take you long to find a curious red bottle lurking in any of our kitchen cupboards.

PLANTAIN

Plantain takes us way back to when we knew it only as dodo—a Yoruba word, not the extinct bird—and it lives on in our memory as a firm favorite. With time we've come to realize that we weren't the only privileged ones, as it's enjoyed in all shapes and seasons across the world. A truly versatile ingredient, it's suitable for breakfast, lunch, or dinner, and as a staple or accompaniment in both in sweet and savory dishes.

Green, yellow, and black are the colors that characterize a plantain's life. When green, it should be handled in much the same way as any other root vegetable, while fried yellow plantain is a sticky treat. Next up on the scale, black plantain is an excellent sweetener when boiled and combined with other ingredients or steamed whole in its skin.

When we think of The Groundnut we always think of plantain. It's the first thing we ever served at our events, and the only constant on the menu. It's a symbolic ingredient for us.

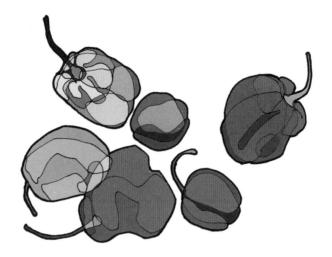

SCOTCH BONNET PEPPER

Scotch bonnets are an important ingredient in our cooking and one of the most distinctive too. Don't be fooled, the green, orange, or red colors give no indication of how spicy they are. If there is a sure technique to perceive the heat of these wonky shaped peppers before you use them, we haven't found it yet. The cute peppers have so much more to them than spice—they are incredibly aromatic and flavorful. When in markets, try to select ones that give off a strong aroma when you get close to them.

Special thanks to:

Aisha, Alice, Anselm, Ana, Guilluame, Ibrahim, Anabelle, Anita, Eleanor, Chris, Rosie, Terry, Fiona, Toby, Reuben, Heather, Arthur & Erica, Auntie Annette, Aunty Harrisat, Becca, Caroline Craig, Clementine, Denis Vraz, Femi, Folaju, Frankie U, Goldsmiths University, Hafssa, Harriet, Ibiye, Issy, Jon Elek, Justin Rangler, Julian Krupski, Katie G, Lauren Chui, Le Bal Café, Lewisham Arthouse, Lindsey, Tamsin & the team at Penguin, Lola B, Lucy & Anthony at Enclave, Manuel, MT, Monica, Moses, Nordine, PLANTAIN, Riaz, Rob Felix, Rosie Lowe, Sandro, Sokari & Alan, Sophie Davidson, The Kabwa family, Toby Glanville. Brixton, Deptford, East Street, Lewisham & Whitechapel markets.

Alcides, Alethea, Anya, Margot, Melanie, JP, Mauricio, Leon, Luis, Pia, Fatima, Alexander Thanni, Alexandra Leese, Auntie Ellen, Big Jo, Emmy Dayal, Emmy Elsmore, Grandad, Grandma (Mrs T), Granny & Grandpa, Henry Stringer, Ibs, Issy, James Browning, Jessica Simmons, Junya, Marina, Julia & Flick, Max Valizadeh, Miles, Mum & Dad, Natasha Robertson, Nicholas Mandalos, Norihiro Usui, Omolarie, Oscar Williams, Serra Tansel, Timothy Ladeji.

Grandma & Uncle Glen, Mummy & the Agustos, Daddy & the Brown family, Aunty Annette, Sister Lola, Papa Daps, Sam Williams, Robert Moore, Anthony Bonsu, Mohammed & Mofe, Aunty Dupe, Aunty Ethel, Aunty Nike, Aunty Molly, Aunty H, Zai & Amina, Chudi & Ikenna, The Mode, Claire Hamilton & Michael Crooks, Kyle, Ininaa, Rosalind, Merrick, Portia, Clubby, Kaspar, Jack & Bossa, Amélie, Ella Bowman, Sam Bailey, Dillon, Gorkan, Tushar, Adam, Agnes Andoh & Daniel Ampaw, Miles Mitchell & family, The Northway family, Sarah Fernandez & family, Eddie & the Livett family, Grahame Clinton, Dr. Thompson, Mr. Joel Smith, Miss Rowling, Branwen Gruffydd Jones, Aoife Mannix, Chinua Achebe.

Amun Osman, Bob & the Fodio family, Dean Stringer, Grandma & Grandpa Todd & the Todd family, Harriet, Joey & the Maxwell-Gumbletons, John Olander & the JB clan, Kate Muwoki, Katy Ideh, Kit, Mich, Jamo & the RVI, Kitty, Felix & Harri, Julie, Nina, Nikos & Kelly, Brendan & Sarah, Hattie, Ollie, Phoebe & Jim, Kojo & the Okudo family, Lani & Marcuse, Matthius Kabuye, Simon, Lena, Dawn.

Love

DUVAL   Folayemi   JACOB

Index by Recipe Type

MEAT & FISH

the Groundnut stew	33
grilled heart	66
kingfish	104
poached chicken	128
pork in tamarind	131
jollof sauce	182
sea bream	216
nyama choma	246
peri-peri chicken	250
tomato stew with guinea fowl	275
anchovy omelette	291

STAPLES

ugali	38
pilau	71
steamed buns	88
steamed plantain	98
tea bread	122
cornmeal noodles	127
fried plantain/dodo	174
baked plantain	177
jollof rice	182
injera pikelet	210
plantain roti	245
yam & plantain scoops	270

SWEETS

pomelo	41
puna yam cake	75
banana almond cake	107
groundnut & almond ice cream	134
avocado & tarragon ice cream	137
stewed plums & loose crumble	141
lady in disguise	185
kiwi ice pop	205
sweet pastry	222
edible fruit bowl	225
pink peppercorn pastille	281
mandazi	253
dried mango	303
papaya	307

EXTRAS

green plantain chips	20
red rub	65
roasted Scotch bonnet & apple sauce	101
Nakuru samosa shells with kidney beans in coconut	121
shito	169
wot	212
granola	304
vegetable stock	313
chicken stock	314
groundnut butter	316
flavored ice cubes	319

Index

Page references in **bold** indicate photographs.

HarperCollins books may be purchased for educational, business, or sales
promotional use. For information please e-mail the Special Markets Department
at SPsales@harpercollins.com.

First published in the UK under the title *The Groundnut Cookbook* by Michael
Joseph, a Penguin Random House company.

FIRST US EDITION

Text copyright © Duval Timothy, Folayemi Brown, and Jacob Fodio Todd.
Photography copyright © 2015 Toby Glanville and Sophie Davidson; pages 221
and 242 © 2015 Lindsey Evans.
Illustration copyright © 2015 Duval Timothy.

Color reproduction by Altaimage, London.

Library of Congress Cataloging-in-Publication Data has been applied for.

ISBN 978-0-06-246740-9

16 17 18 19 20   ID/SCP   10 9 8 7 6 5 4 3 2 1